Mere
APOLOGETICS

APOLOGETICS

How to Help Seekers and Skeptics Find Faith

Alister E. McGrath

BakerBooks

a division of Baker Publishing Group
Grand Rapids, Michigan

© 2012 by Alister E. McGrath

Published by Baker Books
a division of Baker Publishing Group
P.O. Box 6287, Grand Rapids, MI 49516-6287
www.bakerbooks.com

Printed in the United States of America

Library of Congress Cataloging-in-Publication Data
McGrath, Alister E., 1953–
    Mere apologetics : how to help seekers and skeptics find faith / Alister E. McGrath.
        p.   cm.
    Includes bibliographical references and index.
    ISBN 978-0-8010-1416-1 (pbk.)
    1. Apologetics. I. Title.
BT1103.M345 2011
239—dc23   2011029417

12   13   14   15   16   17   18   7   6   5   4   3   2   1

For my colleagues and students at the
Oxford Center for Christian Apologetics

Contents

Introduction

This book is an introduction to apologetics—the field of Christian thought that focuses on the justification of the core themes of the Christian faith and its effective communication to the non-Christian world. It commends a mindset of *engagement*, encouraging Christians to interact with the ideas of our culture rather than running away from them or pretending they can be ignored. Apologetics aims to convert believers into thinkers, and thinkers into believers. It engages our reason, our imagination, and our deepest longings. It opens hearts, eyes, and minds. As the great apologist G. K. Chesterton (1874–1936) once quipped, "The object of opening the mind, as of opening the mouth, is to shut it again on something solid."[1] Apologetics celebrates and proclaims the intellectual solidity, the imaginative richness, and the spiritual depth of the gospel in ways that can connect with our culture.

Apologetics is to be seen not as a defensive and hostile reaction against the world, but as a welcome opportunity to exhibit, celebrate, and display the treasure chest of the Christian faith. It encourages believers to appreciate their faith, and to explain and commend it to those outside the church. It aims to set out the intellectual, moral, imaginative, and relational richness of the Christian faith—partly to reassure believers and help them develop their faith, but primarily to enable those outside the community of faith to realize the compelling vision that lies at the heart of the Christian gospel.

This book sets out to introduce its readers to the leading themes of apologetics, presenting a basic understanding of its agendas and approaches. I have tried to make this book accessible, interesting, and useful, while giving pointers to more advanced resources that will allow you, the reader, to take things further in your own time. It is not comprehensive, so you will need to supplement it with more advanced and specialized texts. Nor is it committed to any particular school of apologetics. Rather than limiting itself to any one specific school or approach to apologetics, this work draws on their collective riches. It aims to encourage and equip its readers to develop an apologetic mindset, and explore further how to explain and commend the gospel to our culture. In many ways, the book's approach mirrors that of C. S. Lewis (1898–1963), perhaps the greatest apologist of the twentieth century. It aims to help you get an idea of what the issues are and how Christians can respond to them. Like any introduction, it will leave you wanting to know more and go further. It cannot hope to answer all of your questions!

All the material used in this book has been tested on student audiences and in public addresses over a period of six years, primarily in a foundational lecture course I teach at the Oxford Center for Christian Apologetics entitled "An Introduction to Christian Apologetics." This has been supplemented by material developed for summer schools in Oxford and at Regent College, Vancouver, dealing with the central themes of apologetics and how they enable the church to engage positively and powerfully with the questions our culture is asking. I am deeply grateful to my students for their feedback, ideas, and stimulus, which have been so important to me in developing the approach set out in this book. I hope it will help others to discover why apologetics is so interesting on the one hand, and so vital to the future of the Christian faith on the other.

Alister McGrath
King's College, London
December 2010

1

Getting Started

What Is Apologetics?

The Great Commission gives every Christian the privilege and responsibility of preaching the Good News until the end of history: "Go and make disciples of all nations" (Matt. 28:18–20 NIV). Every Christian alive today is linked, through a complex chain of historical events, with this pivotal moment. Each of us has a family tree of faith reaching back into the mists of time. Down the ages, like runners in a great relay race of history, others have passed this Good News from one generation to another. And now the baton has been handed to us. It's our turn. We have been entrusted with passing on the Good News to those around and beyond us.

It is an exciting thought. For a start, it helps us to see how we fit into a bigger picture. Yet for many it is also a rather challenging thought. It seems too big a demand. Are we really up for this? How can we cope with such a weighty responsibility? It is important to realize that Christians have always felt overwhelmed by the challenges of passing on our faith. We feel that we lack the wisdom, insight, and strength to do this—and we are right to feel so. But we must appreciate that God knows us, exactly as we are (Ps. 139). He knows our deepest secrets, our strengths, and our weaknesses. And God is able to work in us and through us to speak to the world for which Christ died.

One of the great themes of the Christian Bible is that, whenever God asks us to do something for him, he gives us the gifts we need to do it. Knowing us for what we are, he equips us for what he wants us to do. The Great Commission includes both a command and a promise. The risen Christ's *command* to his disciples is bold and challenging: "Go and make disciples of all nations" (v. 19 NIV). His *promise* to those disciples is equally reassuring and encouraging: "Surely I am with you always, to the very end of the age" (v. 20 NIV). It is a deeply comforting thought. We are not on our own. The risen Christ stands by us and with us, as we do our best to hand on and hand over the Good News of who Christ is and what he has done for us.

Yet knowing that we are accompanied and strengthened in our journey of faith by the risen Christ does not solve the many questions we must face and explore as we commend and proclaim the gospel. How can anyone do justice to the excitement, joy, and wonder of the Christian gospel? Time and time again, we find ourselves unable to express its richness adequately in words. The reality of God and the gospel always exceeds our ability to express it. How can we respond effectively to the questions our culture is asking about God, or the objections it raises to faith? How can we find vivid, faithful, and dynamic ways of explaining and expressing the gospel, allowing it to connect with the hopes and fears of those around us?

How can Christians explain their faith in terms that make sense to people outside the church? How can we counter misunderstandings or misrepresentations of the Christian faith? How can we communicate the truth, attractiveness, and joy of the Christian gospel to our culture? These are questions that have been addressed by Christians since the time of the New Testament. Traditionally, this is known as the discipline of *apologetics*—the subject of this book.

Defining Apologetics

So what is apologetics? Augustine of Hippo (354–430), one of the Christian church's greatest theologians, is widely admired as a biblical interpreter, a preacher, and an expositor of the grace of God. One of his most significant contributions to the development of

Christian theology is his reflections on the doctrine of the Trinity. As readers will know, this doctrine often causes difficulties for people. Augustine, however, had his own problem with the formula "three persons, one God." Why, he complained, did Christians use the word "person" here? It just wasn't helpful. Surely there had to be a better word to use. In the end, Augustine came to the conclusion that there probably wasn't, and the church would just have to keep on using the word "person" in this way.

I often feel like that when using the term "apologetics." It doesn't seem to be a very helpful word. For most people it suggests the idea of "saying you're sorry." Now I am sure there is much that the Christian church needs to say it's sorry about. But that's not really what apologetics is all about. As if that's not enough, the word "apologetics" sounds as if it's plural—but it's really singular (like "scissors"). Yet while Christian writers have sought alternative terms down the ages, none really seems to have caught on. We're just going to have to keep on using "apologetics." But if we can't change the word, we can make sure we understand its richness of meaning.

The term "apologetics" makes a lot more sense when we consider the meaning of the Greek word on which it is based—*apologia*. An *apologia* is a "defense," a reasoned case proving the innocence of an accused person in court, or a demonstration of the correctness of an argument or belief. We find this term used in 1 Peter 3:15, which many see as a classic biblical statement of the importance of apologetics:

> In your hearts set apart Christ as Lord. Always be prepared to give an answer [*apologia*] to everyone who asks you to give the reason [*logos*] for the hope that you have. But do this with gentleness and respect. (NIV)

It is an important text, worth reading in its full context. The first letter of Peter is addressed to Christians in the region of the Roman Empire known as Asia Minor (modern-day Turkey). Peter offers them reassurance and comfort as they face the threat of persecution. He encourages them to engage their critics and questioners by explaining the basis and content of their faith with gentleness and respect.

Peter clearly assumes that Christian ideas are being misunderstood or misrepresented, and urges his readers to set the record
straight—but to do so graciously and considerately. For Peter,
apologetics is about defending the truth with gentleness and respect. The object of apologetics is not to antagonize or humiliate
those outside the church, but to help open their eyes to the reality,
reliability, and relevance of the Christian faith. There must be no
mismatch or contradiction between the message that is proclaimed
and the tone of the messenger's proclamation. We must be win-
some, generous, and gracious. If the gospel is to cause difficulty,
it must be on account of its intrinsic nature and content, not the
manner in which it is proclaimed.[1] It is one thing for the gospel to
give offense; it is quite another for its defenders to cause offense
by unwise choice of language or an aggressive and dismissive attitude toward outsiders.

Christians have taken this advice seriously from the earliest days
of the church. The New Testament itself contains several important passages—mostly in the Acts of the Apostles—that explain,
commend, and defend the Christian faith to a variety of audiences. For example, Peter's famous sermon on the day of Pentecost
argues that Jesus of Nazareth is the culmination of the hopes of
Israel (Acts 2). Paul's equally famous sermon to the philosophers
of Athens argues that Jesus of Nazareth is the culmination of the
long human quest for wisdom (Acts 17).

This engagement continued throughout the history of the church.
Early Christian writers were especially concerned to engage Platonism. How could they communicate the truth and power of the
gospel to an audience used to thinking in Platonic ways? This approach involved the identification of both possibilities and challenges, leading to the exploitation of those possibilities and the
neutralization of those challenges. Yet Platonism generally fell out
of fashion in the early Middle Ages. Aristotle became the philosopher of choice in most western universities from the thirteenth
century until the early sixteenth century. Once more, Christian
apologists rose to this challenge. They identified the challenges
raised by Aristotelianism—such as its belief in the eternity of the
world. And they also identified the openings it created for faith.
That task continues today, as we face new intellectual and cultural

challenges and opportunities. It is easy to feel overwhelmed by the challenges arising from cultural changes—and so fail to see the opportunities they offer.

The Basic Themes of Christian Apologetics

Before exploring these possibilities, we need to think a little more about the nature of apologetics. What issues does it engage? How does it help us proclaim and communicate the gospel? We could summarize the three tasks faced by apologists of the past and present under three main headings: defending, commending, and translating.

Defending

Here, the apologist sets out to find the barriers to faith. Have they arisen through misunderstandings or misrepresentations? If so, these need to be corrected. Have they arisen because of a genuine difficulty over Christian truth claims? If so, these need to be addressed. It is important to note that defense is generally a reactive strategy. Someone comes up with a concern; we are obliged to respond to it. Happily, there are excellent responses that can be made, and the apologist needs to know and understand these. Where honest questions are sincerely asked, honest answers must be powerfully yet graciously given.

Yet everyone has different questions, concerns, and anxieties. As a result, the apologist needs to know her audience. What are the difficulties people experience with the Christian gospel? One of the first things that the apologist learns when he does apologetics—as opposed to just reading books about it—is that audiences vary enormously. Each person has his or her own specific difficulties about faith and must not be reduced to a generalized stereotype.

These difficulties are often intellectual, concerning questions about the evidential basis for faith or some core Christian doctrines. But it is important to realize that not all of these difficulties fall into this category. Some are much deeper concerns, and are not so much about problems with rational understanding as about problems with existential commitment. French apologist Blaise Pascal (1623–62) once perceptively commented: "The heart has its reasons, which reason knows nothing about." Apologetics aims to identify these barriers to faith, whatever their nature, and offer responses that help to overcome them.

Apologetics thus encourages Christians to develop a "discipleship of the mind." Before we can answer the questions others ask us about our faith, we need to have answered them for ourselves. Christ calls on his followers to love God with all their heart, with all their soul, and with all their mind (Matt. 22:37). Paul also speaks about the renewal of our minds (Rom. 12:2) as part of the process of transforming our lives. To be a Christian is to think about our faith, beginning to forge answers to our own questions. Apologetics is about going further and deeper into the Christian faith, discovering its riches. It's good for our own appreciation of the richness and reasonableness of our faith. But, perhaps just as importantly, it enables us to deal with the questions that others have.

It is also important to appreciate that it is not just people outside the church who are asking questions about faith. Many Christians also experience difficulties with their faith and find themselves looking for explanations or approaches that will help them sustain it. While the primary focus of apologetics may indeed be culture at large, we must never forget that many Christians need help with their faith. Why does God allow suffering? How can I make sense of the Trinity? Will my pets go to heaven when they die? These are all apologetic questions familiar to any pastor. And they need to be answered. Happily, there are indeed answers that are deeply rooted in the long Christian tradition of engaging Scripture.

It is important for Christians to show that they understand these concerns, and don't see them simply as arguments to be lightly and easily dismissed. We need to deal with them sensitively and compassionately, entering into the mind of the person who finds them a problem. Why is it a problem? What have you seen that they haven't? How can you help them see things in a new way that either neutralizes the problem or makes it clear this is a problem they're already well used to in other areas of life? It is important not to be dismissive, but gracious and sympathetic. Apologetics is as much about our personal attitudes and character as it is about our arguments and analysis. You can defend the gospel without being defensive in your attitude.

Commending

Here, the apologist sets out to allow the truth and relevance of the gospel to be appreciated by the audience. The audience may be a single person or a large group of people. In each case, the apologist will try to allow the full wonder and brilliance of the Christian faith to be understood and appreciated. The gospel does not need to be made relevant to these audiences. The question is how we help the audience grasp this relevance—for example, by using helpful illustrations, analogies, or stories that allow them to connect with it.

Apologetics thus has a strongly positive dimension—setting out the full attractiveness of Jesus Christ so that those outside the faith can begin to grasp why he merits such serious consideration. Christ himself once compared the kingdom of heaven to a pearl of great price: "The kingdom of heaven is like a merchant looking for fine pearls. When he found one of great value, he went away and sold everything he had and bought it" (Matt. 13:45–46 NIV). The merchant knew about pearls, and he could see that this particular pearl was so beautiful and valuable it was worth giving up everything so he could possess it.

As we shall see, one classic way of doing this is to show that Christianity is rationally compelling. It makes better sense of things than its rivals. Yet it is vitally important not to limit the appeal of the gospel to human reason. What of the human heart? Time after time, the Gospels tell us people were drawn to Jesus of Nazareth because they realized he could transform their lives. While arguments are important in apologetics, they have their limits. Many are attracted to the Christian faith today because of their belief that it will change their lives. Their criterion of validation is not so much "Is this true?" but "Will this work?"

Our task is to help people realize that the Christian faith is so exciting and wonderful that nothing else can compare to it. This means helping people grasp the attractiveness of the faith. Theology allows us to identify and appreciate the individual elements of the Christian faith. It is like someone opening a treasure chest and holding up jewels, pearls, and precious metals, one by one, so that each may be seen individually and appreciated. It is like holding a diamond up to the light, so that each of its facets scintillates, allowing its beauty and glory to be appreciated.

Translating

Here, the apologist recognizes that many of the core ideas and themes of the Christian faith are likely to be unfamiliar to many audiences. They need to be explained using familiar or accessible images, terms, or stories. C. S. Lewis is rightly regarded as a master of this skill, and his estimation of its importance must be taken to heart:

> We must learn the language of our audience. And let me say at the outset that it is no use laying down *a priori* what the "plain man" does or does not understand. You have to find out by experience. . . . You must translate every bit of your theology into the vernacular. . . . I have come to the conclusion that if you cannot translate your own thoughts into uneducated language, then your thoughts are confused. Power to translate is the test of having really understood your own meaning.[2]

The issue here is about how we faithfully and effectively communicate the Christian faith to a culture that may not understand traditional Christian terms or concepts. We need to be able to set out and explain the deep attraction of the Christian gospel for our culture, using language and images it can access. It is no accident that Christ used parables to teach about the kingdom of God. He used language and imagery already familiar to the rural Palestinian culture of his age to communicate deeper spiritual truths.

So how can we translate core ideas of the Christian faith—such as redemption and salvation—into the cultural vernacular? Biblical terms need to be explained and interpreted if they are to resonate with where people are today. An example will make this point clearer. Paul declares that "since we have been justified through faith, we have peace with God through our Lord Jesus Christ" (Rom. 5:1 NIV). This is clearly a statement of a core element of the Christian gospel. But it will not be understood by contemporary audiences, who will probably misunderstand Paul's central notion of "justification" in one of two ways:

1. A defense of our integrity or "rightness," in the sense of "I provided a justification of my actions to my employers." It's about showing that we are right.

2. The alignment of the text against the right-hand margin of a document, particularly when word processing. It's about straightening up a ragged text.

Neither of these really illuminates Paul's meaning in Romans 5:1; indeed, it could be argued that both definitions are likely to mislead people about his intentions and concerns. Paul's idea of justification thus needs to be explained in terms that are both faithful to his original intention and intelligible to contemporary audiences. One might, for example, begin to explain this by talking about being "put right" with God, allowing both the relational and judicial aspects of the concept of justification to be explored.

From what has been said thus far, it is clear that apologetics is concerned with three themes, each of which brings new depth to our personal faith and a new quality to our Christian witness:

1. Identifying and responding to objections or difficulties concerning the gospel, and helping to overcome these barriers to faith.
2. Communicating the excitement and wonder of the Christian faith, so that its potential to transform the human situation can be appreciated.
3. Translating the core ideas of the Christian faith into language that makes sense to outsiders.

We shall be considering each of these issues in greater depth later in the book. We now need to consider how apologetics relates to evangelism.

Apologetics and Evangelism

From what has just been said, it can be seen that Christian apologetics represents a serious and sustained engagement with the "ultimate questions" raised by a culture, people group, or individual, aiming to show how the Christian faith is able to provide meaningful answers to such questions. Where is God in the suffering of the world? Is faith in God reasonable? Apologetics clears the ground for evangelism, just as John the Baptist prepared the way for the coming of Jesus of Nazareth.

Evangelism moves beyond this attempt to demonstrate the cultural plausibility of the Christian faith. Where apologetics can be considered to clear the ground for faith in Christ, evangelism invites people to respond to the gospel. Where apologetics aims to secure *consent*, evangelism aims to secure *commitment*. David Bosch's influential and widely accepted definition of evangelism makes this point well:

> Evangelism is the proclamation of salvation in Christ to those who do not believe in him, calling them to repentance and conversion, announcing forgiveness of sins, and inviting them to become living members of Christ's earthly community and to begin a life of service to others in the power of the Holy Spirit.[3]

Developing this same approach, we might say that apologetics aims to establish the plausibility of salvation in Christ—for example, by developing an intellectual case based on cultural history for the fallenness or sinfulness of humanity, or by appealing to the experience of spiritual longing as a sign of alienation from God and our true destiny. The task of apologetics is therefore to prepare the way for the coming of Christ, just as someone might clear rocks and other roadblocks from a pathway.

The dividing line between apologetics and evangelism is fuzzy; making a distinction between them, however, is helpful. Apologetics is conversational, where evangelism is invitational.[4] While an apologetic conversation about the Christian faith can easily lead into an invitation to faith, it is much more concerned with removing misunderstandings, explaining ideas, and exploring the personal relevance of faith. Apologetics is about persuading people that there is a door to another world—a door that perhaps they never realized existed. Evangelism is about helping people to open that door and enter into the new world that lies beyond.

A rough working definition of evangelism might be "inviting someone to become a Christian." Apologetics could then be thought of as clearing the ground for that invitation so that it is more likely to receive a positive response. Or again, evangelism could be said to be like offering someone bread. Apologetics would then be about persuading people there is bread to be had and it is good to eat.

An example may help make this point clearer. Jesus of Nazareth often compared the kingdom of God to a feast (Luke 14:15–24). Apologetics can be thought of as explaining to people that there really is going to be a feast. It invites them to reflect on what they might find there—the food and the drink. How wonderful it would be to be invited! If only this were true! As Blaise Pascal once quipped, we must "make good people wish that [the Christian faith] were true, and then show that it is."[5] Pascal's point is that we ought to help people long for what the Christian faith promises—and then show them it is indeed true and real. The desire for something provides the motivation to check it out.

Evangelism is different. It issues a personal invitation: "You are invited to the feast! Please come!" Apologetics lays the ground for this invitation; evangelism extends it. Both are an essential part of the mission of the church. Apologetics establishes and proclaims the plausibility and desirability of the gospel; evangelism summons people to enter into it and share in its benefits. Apologetics is not evangelism, and is inadequate without it. Yet it has an important and distinct role to play in the Christian community's engagement with the world, as well as in encouraging and developing the faith of Christian believers.

However, there are potential difficulties with apologetics that need to be identified. Every tool needs to be calibrated to make sure that we understand its strengths and weaknesses. We need to know the conditions under which it works well, and when it is likely to go wrong. We shall consider this matter in the next section.

The Limitations of Apologetics

When properly understood and properly used, apologetics is of vital importance to the ministry of the church. It can bring a new quality and intellectual depth to the life of ordinary believers, equipping them to answer their own questions about their faith and those asked by their friends. And it helps us build bridges to our culture, preparing the way for the gospel proclamation. Yet apologetics can easily be misunderstood and just as easily misapplied.

One of the things apologetics aims to do is translate key ideas of the Christian faith into categories the world can understand. For example, some biblical terms—such as justification—need to be interpreted to secular culture, as they are liable to be misunderstood. Yet although this process of "cultural translation" of key gospel ideas can be enormously important in helping people understand what the Christian faith is all about, it can lead to two unhelpful outcomes.

First, translation into cultural terms can easily lead to Christian ideas being reduced to their cultural equivalents. For example, it is helpful to think of Jesus Christ as the mediator between humanity and God, and there is excellent New Testament warrant for speaking of Christ in this way. It helps identify what is so important about Christ from a Christian perspective. Yet modern western culture understands a "mediator" in a professional sense—someone experienced at conflict resolution who is asked to sort out a dispute between two parties. Speaking of Jesus Christ as mediator risks reducing his role to what contemporary culture understands by the idea—for example, Jesus as the peacemaker. We need to make sure we do not reduce Jesus Christ or the Christian gospel to terms our culture can understand. Apologetics can lead to loss of distinctive Christian identity.

This can, of course, be avoided by making it clear that apologetics is aiming to establish bridges with contemporary culture. In the end, the gospel is not something that can or should be reduced to western cultural norms. Rather, it is something whose truth and relevance can be more effectively communicated through the judicious choice and use of cultural analogies, values, or stories. But it is not the same as any of these. We can use phrases such as "It's a bit like . . ." But in the end, we have to realize that the gospel transcends and transforms any and all cultural ideas we may use as channels for its communication. These are vehicles and channels for the gospel; they are not the gospel itself.

Second, apologetics runs the risk of creating the impression that showing the reasonableness of faith is all that is required. This is one of the reasons to emphasize the importance of evangelism. To use an analogy found in the writings of Martin Luther, faith is like getting into a boat and crossing the sea to an island. Apologetics can help establish that it is reasonable to believe there is a boat, that it is likely to be safe to travel in, and that there is an island just beyond the horizon. But you still need to get in the boat and travel to the island. Faith is about commitment to God, not just belief in God. Once more, this is a difficulty that can be avoided by realizing apologetics and evangelism are essential and interconnected partners in Christian outreach.

Moving On

In this opening chapter, we have reflected on some basic themes of Christian apologetics. How are we to relate the Christian faith to contemporary culture? As we shall see at various points throughout this work, one of the best ways of doing this is to make sure we have really understood the Christian faith, and appreciated its intellectual, relational, aesthetic, imaginative, and ethical appeal. There is much to appreciate!

Yet we also need to reflect on the cultural context within which we proclaim, explain, and commend the gospel. People do not exist in cultural vacuums. They live in a specific situation, and often absorb at least some of its ideas and values. In the next chapter, we shall begin to reflect on the role played by culture in apologetics.

For Further Reading

Craig, William Lane. *Reasonable Faith: Christian Truth and Apologetics*, 3rd ed. Wheaton: Crossway, 2008.

Kreeft, Peter, and Ronald K. Tacelli. *Handbook of Catholic Apologetics: Reasoned Answers to Questions of Faith*. San Francisco: Ignatius Press, 2009.

Markos, Louis. *Apologetics for the Twenty-First Century*. Wheaton: Crossway, 2010.

Peters, James R. *The Logic of the Heart: Augustine, Pascal, and the Rationality of Faith*. Grand Rapids: Baker Academic, 2009.

Sire, James W. *A Little Primer on Humble Apologetics*. Downers Grove, IL: InterVarsity, 2006.

Sproul, R. C. *Defending Your Faith: An Introduction to Apologetics*. Wheaton: Crossway, 2003.

Stackhouse, John G. *Humble Apologetics: Defending the Faith Today*. Oxford: Oxford University Press, 2002.

Taylor, James E. *Introducing Apologetics: Cultivating Christian Commitment*. Grand Rapids: Baker Academic, 2006.

2

Apologetics and Contemporary Culture

FROM MODERNITY TO POSTMODERNITY

pologetics always takes place within a specific cultural context. Christian missionaries to China and India soon discovered that the apologetic methods that seemed to work well in western Europe did not seem to be effective in Asia. It was necessary to develop new approaches that resonated with the cultural mood and patterns of thought characteristic of these regions. An apologetic approach that was very productive in one context might prove much less effective, and perhaps even counterproductive, in a different cultural environment.

Apologetics and Modernity

The dominant cultural environment of the West, from about 1750 to 1960, is usually defined as "modernity." This outlook was shaped by a belief in a universal human reason, common to all people and times, capable of gaining access to the deeper structures of the world. Reason was the key that unlocked the mysteries of life, and argument was its tool of persuasion. Rational argument became the trusted tool of this cultural age. Christian apologists rapidly realized the importance of this development. The rational defense of the Christian faith became of paramount importance.

The types of apologetics Christian writers developed to engage modernity focused on demonstrating the logical and rational grounds of faith. True beliefs were based on correct assumptions, which were in turn based on rational rules of logic. Apologetics was thus primarily conceived as arguments based on logic, appealing to the human mind. While these approaches had many strengths, they nevertheless neglected the relational, imaginative, and existential aspects of faith. As we noted earlier, French philosopher and Christian apologist Blaise Pascal famously complained about this excessive focus on reason. What about the human heart? The heart had its own reasons for believing, he declared, which reason could not grasp.

One important result of the impact of rationalism on Christian apologetics was the downplaying of any aspects of Christian thought that were seen as "irrational" or "illogical"—such as the doctrine of the Trinity. Few eighteenth- or nineteenth-century Christian apologists defended this idea, believing it was something of a liability in the face of the hard rationalism dominating this age. The rediscovery of the theological importance of the doctrine of the Trinity and the birth of a new confidence in its foundations and coherence dates from after World War I, when the easy assumptions of Enlightenment rationalism had been dealt a significant blow by the irrationality of the First World War.

Yet Christian apologists generally responded well to the challenges of rationalism, and developed new approaches to apologetics that chimed in with the "spirit of the age." This age produced some landmark works of apologetics. Edward John Carnell (1919–67) produced a work that became a classic evangelical reasoned defense of the Christian faith.[1] Yet the passing of time has made the continued use of such works problematic, for two reasons:

1. Each age generates its own specific concerns and critiques of the Christian faith. Many of the issues seen as important by Carnell and other apologists of this age now seem of little significance. Indeed, reading older works of apologetics often seems like a journey down memory lane, marked by the names of writers and controversies that no longer seem relevant.

2. Many apologists of modernity engaged their cultural context using approaches they believed would resonate with their audiences—such as an appeal to rational argument as the basis for a trustworthy faith. As we shall see, the hallmark of good apologetics is an ability to engage specific audiences. Yet the modernist assumption of the primacy of rationality has now been called into question, raising difficulties for apologetic approaches based upon or appealing to it.

One of the problems here is that rationalist approaches to apologetics tend to minimize the element of mystery within the Christian faith in order to make Christianity appear more accessible to reason. Yet the Christian gospel expresses some God-given ideas that lie far beyond the capacity of the human mind to discover by itself. In trying to win arguments with particular opponents, apologists sometimes buy into the assumptions of their adversaries. A tactical advantage can easily become a strategic liability. The danger of forms of apologetics that respond to rationalism is that they often end up importing rationalism into Christianity, rather than exporting the gospel into a rationalist culture.

The Rise of Postmodernity

In the early twenty-first century, western Christianity faces a cultural context more complex and varied than that known by apologists in the middle of the twentieth century. Individuals and Christian communities live in a postmodern world. The apologetic approaches that seemed to work so well in the 1950s and early 1960s seem out of tune with the cultural mood of a later generation.

The term "postmodernism" first made its appearance around 1971. It was initially used to refer to a new architectural style, but was soon applied to the world of ideas. Postmodernism came to refer to the growing cultural belief that modernity had failed and needed to be corrected. This feeling initially focused on the failures of "modern art" to engage with the human imagination, but rapidly extended to social issues and problems arising from a naïve belief in the inevitability of progress—such as the growth of industrialization

and urbanization. It is important to note that this emerging movement did not choose to style itself "antimodernism." Postmodernism is not a rejection of every aspect of modernity, but is seen by
its advocates as an attempt to combine the best of the modern
world with the best elements of classical traditions and eliminate
the undesirable aspects of both.

Postmodernity has been severely criticized for its intellectual
shallowness, especially its eclecticism. Who decides what we pick
and mix from the past and the present? Postmodern authors, on the
other hand, argue that the movement represents an attempt to move
society and thought forward in a way that utilizes the best insights
of the past but is not trapped by it. One of their main concerns
is to fight the vast "totalizing schemes"—such as Marxism—that
were so typical of modernity, and are now seen to constitute an
intellectual and cultural straightjacket. As we shall see presently,
this critique of such "uniformitarianism" is of major importance
to Christian apologetics.

So how do we respond to this major cultural shift? Perhaps the
first step is to get a sense of proportion about this development.
Reflecting on the history of the church allows us to see this shift
in its proper perspective. Every generation believes it stands at a
critical point in history. Augustine of Hippo, writing in the early
fifth century, remarked on how many people of his time longed for
the good old days, when Christianity was given support and security
by the Roman Empire. Bernard of Clairvaux, writing seven hundred
years later, wrote of the sense of nostalgia many then felt for the
time of Augustine. And many sixteenth-century writers commented
on how much they longed to have lived at the time of Bernard of
Clairvaux. Things were so much better then! We find it very easy to
believe things were better in the past. We must remember that the
past is easily idealized and romanticized, especially by those who
feel alienated and displaced in the present.

Yet our task is not to be nostalgic about the past, but to deal with
the challenges of the present, making use of past approaches to
apologetics when they are helpful (as they so often are). Apologetics
always takes place against a shifting cultural context. The gospel
remains the same; the questions asked about it and the challenges
it faces vary hugely from one cultural location to another. The

tide of modernism swept in and is now receding. Postmodernism now seems dominant. But in a generation's time, things may well seem very different.

There is no need for Christian apologists to be alarmed by the rise of postmodernity. The Christian faith possesses ample resources to meet this challenge. It's just that we haven't used some of them for generations, as they seemed inappropriate in a modernist worldview. The rise of postmodernity certainly brings some real challenges for Christian apologetics; yet it is clear that it brings some equally real opportunities. It is also clear that this new cultural mood offers challenges to churches in that it forces them to do some significant rethinking. Is this way of preaching the Christian gospel really the best way to do it? Is it too deeply embedded in an earlier worldview, so that it falls with modernity's passing?

For many younger western apologists, Christianity seems to have become deeply enmeshed within the plausibility structures of modernity, that great period in European cultural history regnant from about 1750 to 1960. The rise of postmodernism thus provides the occasion for a review of this development. What some older writers seem to regard as theologically necessary may simply turn out to have been culturally convenient or historically contingent.

So how are we to explain, defend, or communicate the Christian gospel in this changing cultural situation? While I believe postmodernism is actually quite difficult to defend and sustain intellectually, I nevertheless accept that it continues to shape cultural perceptions. We have to connect with where people are, not with where we think they ought to be. In any case, I also believe it gives us new opportunities to preach and communicate the gospel, as I hope to show.

Some older apologists seem to think the best way of proclaiming the gospel in a postmodern context is to try and get people to go back to modernity. This is neither right nor possible. In this book, I will neither defend nor criticize either modernity or postmodernity. I shall simply take them as cultural "givens" shaped by the happenstances of history, and assume it is evident that both have their points of strength and of vulnerability. Postmodernity certainly offers us some challenges—but I believe they are challenges to which churches can rise, and from which they may benefit.

Apologetics and Postmodernity

So what are the core themes of this "postmodernism" of which we are speaking? It has become something of a sacred tradition to begin any reflections on how the church should live and witness in postmodernity with a detailed account of scholarly reflections on the historical emergence, philosophical roots, and cultural implications of postmodernism, sprinkled with judicious hints that the term is ultimately fluid and probably even elusive. Nevertheless, it is clear that something significant has happened in western culture during the last generation, even if its precise description remains hard to pin down.

Perhaps the most distinctive feature of postmodernism is its rejection of what I shall call uniformitarianism—that is, the insistence that there is only one right way of thinking and only one right way of behaving. Postmodern writers see such attitudes as underlying Nazism and Stalinism, which they regard as the unacceptable public face of uniformitarianism. A demand for uniformity is held to lead to repression in that people are forced to fit into one single preconceived mold. To use the language of some leading postmodern philosophers, "the other" is relentlessly reduced to "the same."

Postmodernism can be seen as a reaction against these ways of thinking, which it regards as oppressive. In their place, a cultural mood has developed that celebrates diversity and seeks to undermine those who offer rigid, restrictive, and oppressive views of the world. It reacts primarily against modernism, which tried to reduce everything to a uniform set of ideas. This is seen as an attempt to control and master other people, a form of intellectual or cultural Stalinism, characterized by its refusal to permit diversity in our readings of the world. Human freedom, it is suggested, is dependent upon successfully identifying, challenging, and ultimately subverting such controlling "metanarratives."

Yet it is fair to point out that postmodernism has its own family of distinct metanarratives, which are far from being above criticism. Indeed, some of these metanarratives have become the regnant orthodoxy within at least certain sections of western culture, raising fundamental questions for those who disagree with the "big picture" of reality it proposes. For example, consider the relativist who maintains that all points of view on a given topic are equally valid, even though they are apparently incompatible. This stance is ultimately grounded in an underlying understanding of reality (we might say a "narrative of reality" or metanarrative) that comes into clear and explicit conflict with other narratives of reality that regard reality as open, at least in principle, to public experience and discussion.

It is, in fact, not easy to give a definition of what postmodernity actually is. Its leading interpreters view it in quite different ways; indeed, some would say it is intrinsically and necessarily resistant to any form of definition. The best we can hope to do is to offer a description, or some kind of sketch, of postmodernity. In what follows, I shall draw on an illuminating and perceptive recent account of the leading themes of postmodernity from the pen of Kevin Vanhoozer, a leading evangelical theologian based at Wheaton College, Illinois.[2]

Vanhoozer suggests that the complex phenomenon of postmodernity can be summarized in terms of four criticisms it directs against older ways of thinking:

1. *Reason.* Vanhoozer notes that the modern approach of reasoning by argument is viewed with suspicion by postmodern writers. Where modernity believed in a single universal reason, postmodernity holds that there are many different kinds of rationality. "They deny the notion of universal rationality; reason is rather a contextual and relative affair."

2. *Truth.* Postmodernity, Vanhoozer argues, is suspicious of the idea of truth because of the way in which it has been used to legitimate oppression, or give justification to vested interests. Truth, on this view, is "a compelling story told by persons in positions of power in order to perpetuate their way of seeing and organizing the natural and social world."

3. *History.* Where modern writers tried to find universal patterns in history, Vanhoozer suggests that postmodernity is "incredulous towards narratives that purport to recount universal history." From the standpoint of Christian apologetics, this means that any attempt to see universal significance in

the narrative of Jesus of Nazareth will be viewed with intense suspicion by some in today's culture.

4. *Self*. Following on from this, Vanhoozer notes how postmodernity rejects any notion there is "one true way of recounting one's own history" and thus concludes there is "no true way of narrating one's own identity." All ways of understanding the individual are open-ended and partial. There is no universal answer to the question of human identity.

Vanhoozer's analysis is important, as it helps identify the stumbling blocks and suspicions some older approaches to Christian apologetics will encounter in postmodern contexts. Yet it is essential to appreciate two points:

1. Postmodernity must never be thought of as defining what is "right" or "true." It is a cultural mood, shaped by certain values and beliefs. Like modernity, postmodernity is an essentially secular outlook, neither anti- nor pro-Christian. It simply describes a cultural context within which we must do apologetics.

2. Many of the approaches to apologetics that we describe as "traditional" are actually quite recent creations and represent responses to a modernist context. Apologists who wanted to engage modernity developed approaches specifically adapted to modernist assumptions—above all, the priority of reason.

We must realize we are free to develop apologetic approaches that are faithful to the Christian gospel on the one hand, and are adapted to our own cultural situation on the other. By doing this, we are repeating the method of "traditional apologetics" while responding to the changes in the cultural context toward which it is directed. We simply cannot use an apologetic approach developed to engage eighteenth-century rationalism to defend the faith to twenty-first-century people who regard rationalism as outdated and constricting!

For example, postmodernity finds appeals to rational argument problematic. But it is deeply attracted to stories and images. Furthermore, postmodernity is more interested in a truth that proves itself capable of being lived out than being demonstrated by rational argument. This helps us understand why "incarnational apologetics," which emphasizes the apologetic importance of faithful living, has become so influential in recent years. As will become clear in a later chapter, we can easily rise to this new challenge, usually not by inventing new approaches to apologetics, but by recovering older approaches that the rise of rationalism seemed to make obsolete.

As we shall see, the rise of postmodernity may change some of the approaches we adopt—but it does not invalidate the tasks or intellectual foundations of Christian apologetics. The fundamental principles remain what they always have been:

1. Understand the Christian gospel.
2. Understand the context within which you are doing apologetics.
3. Develop apologetic approaches that are faithful to the gospel and build on the "common ground" or "points of contact" with the cultural context.

The Approach Adopted in This Book

There are many different ways of doing apologetics. Some books use a "case study" approach, considering a number of objections or difficulties concerning the Christian faith. Each of these is then examined, and answers are offered. Other books appeal to the historical or rational evidence for faith. Others suggest that the world simply cannot be understood without reference to God. This book does not reflect the approach of any school of apologetics, but aims to equip its users to think apologetically, drawing on the best apologists to help explore the issues.

The basic approach of this book can be summarized in the following sequence of steps. Each of these will be explored in much greater detail later. At this stage, I am simply introducing them.

1. Understand the faith.

First, it is essential to have a good understanding of the Christian faith. This knowledge of the gospel, however, needs to be focused apologetically. We need to reflect on how the leading themes of faith can connect with people and engage with their experiences and ideas. This means trying to adopt an "outsider perspective" on faith, asking how an unbeliever might respond to core aspects of the gospel instead of focusing on the kind of discussions Christians might have among themselves.

For example, a biblical scholar might ask: "How does the parable of the Prodigal Son help us understand the relation of Jesus of Nazareth to Judaism?" The apologist asks a rather different question: "How does this parable help us relate to the world of the unbeliever?" The apologist will want to explore how the ideas, narratives, and images of faith can engage with the realities of everyday life.

2. Understand the audience.

Second, it is important to understand the audience being addressed. Who are they? My own experience is that audiences vary enormously—as they did in New Testament times. Compare the radically different approaches of Peter when addressing an audience of Jews (Acts 2) and Paul when addressing a Greek audience (Acts 17). The same gospel is commended and communicated in quite different ways, tailored to the worlds of those very different groups of people. Each audience has its own questions, objections, and difficulties that need to be engaged, just as it has its own "points of contact" and openings for faith.

To give some obvious examples: our audiences have huge variations in knowledge of the Christian faith. Some audiences have no knowledge of the Bible, and regard it as an irrelevance. Others retain a memory and affection for some biblical passages, such as Psalm 23:1, "The Lord is my shepherd." Audiences have quite different cultural locations. Some have very modern perspectives; others are postmodern. Some love classic works of literature; others prefer to talk about the most recent shows on television. Some use very abstract ways of thinking; others think in terms of images or stories. In each case, we are forced to think about how we can best communicate the Christian faith in terms that will resonate with the experience and knowledge of our audience.

3. Communicate with clarity.

Third, we must translate our faith into a language that can be understood by our audiences. The great debates over biblical translation can help us here, as they focus our attention on the need to *communicate* its message to contemporary people. As C. S. Lewis wisely remarked: "Our business is to present that which is timeless (the same yesterday, today, and tomorrow—Heb. 13:8) in the particular language of our own age."[3] Our privilege and responsibility is to express the timeless truths of the gospel using language and imagery adapted to our audiences. The apologist is thus someone who translates the realities of faith into the cultural vernacular.

4. Find points of contact.

Fourth, we need to identify points of contact for the gospel that are already embedded in human culture and experience. God has not left himself without a witness in history, culture, or human experience (Acts 14:17). Our task is to try to identify that witness (whether in nature, society, or a moral code), and use it as a point of contact for the proclamation of the Christian gospel.

5. Present the whole gospel.

Fifth, we must make sure we do not impoverish the appeal of the Christian faith by restricting it to what we personally enjoy or find attractive. C. S. Lewis emphasized how the apologist must make a scrupulous distinction between the "Christian message" and "one's own ideas." If we fail to make this distinction, what is presented to our audiences is not the Christian gospel but those aspects of the gospel we happen to regard as important and interesting. For Lewis, the temptation to focus on what we personally like or approve simply impoverishes the gospel. We end up promoting ourselves—when we are meant to be promoting Christ.

Nevertheless, the impact of the Christian faith upon our lives is itself important apologetically. Why? Because it witnesses to the capacity of the gospel to transform existence. Lewis's point is that we must avoid presenting Christianity simply in terms of our personal preferences and focus instead on identifying its capacity to engage the deepest levels of human existence—our hearts, minds, and souls.

Nor must we needlessly inhibit the appeal of Christianity by limiting the means by which we communicate it. Many in western Christianity focus on its core ideas and see apologetics as the rational defense of Christian truth claims. Now let me make it clear that this is correct, as far as it goes. But this is not the whole truth. We need to go further, noticing how Scripture uses images, stories, and ideas to communicate its core message. For example, Jesus of Nazareth used parables to communicate the great themes of the kingdom of God. These stories were able to plant some core ideas in the minds of his audiences. How can we do the same today?

6. Practice, practice, practice.

Sixth, apologetics is not just about theory; it's about practice. We need to be able to apply apologetic ideas and approaches in everyday life—in conversations, debates, interviews, or whatever interactions we have with other people. Apologetics is both a *science* and an *art*. It is not just about knowledge; it is about wisdom. It's like a skilled and experienced medical practitioner, who knows the theory of medicine well. But she has to apply it to her patients, and that means learning how to relate to them—how to help them tell her what the real problems are, finding ways of communicating technical medical terms in ordinary language, and explaining how they can be addressed.

These six themes will be explored throughout the following chapters, as we reflect on the great themes and approaches of Christian apologetics.

Moving On

We have looked briefly at some initial questions concerning apologetics. The scene is set for a much fuller discussion that follows, where we will explore some of these themes in greater detail. We begin by considering the deep theological foundations on which Christian apologetics rests.

For Further Reading

Allen, Diogenes. *Christian Belief in a Postmodern World: The Full Wealth of Conviction*. Louisville: Westminster John Knox, 1989.

Craig, William Lane. *Reasonable Faith: Christian Truth and Apologetics*, 3rd ed. Wheaton: Crossway, 2008.

Middleton, J. Richard, and Brian J. Walsh. *Truth Is Stranger Than It Used to Be. Biblical Faith in a Postmodern Age*. Downers Grove, IL: InterVarsity, 1995.

Newbigin, Lesslie. *Truth to Tell: The Gospel as Public Truth*. Grand Rapids: Eerdmans, 1991.

Sire, James W. *Naming the Elephant: Worldview as a Concept*. Downers Grove, IL: InterVarsity, 2004.

Vanhoozer, Kevin J., ed., *The Cambridge Companion to Postmodern Theology*. Cambridge: Cambridge University Press, 2003.

3

The Theological Basis
of Apologetics

*A*pologetics is not a set of techniques for winning people to Christ. It is not a set of argumentative templates designed to win debates. It is a willingness to work with God in helping people discover and turn to his glory. As Avery Dulles once noted with some sadness, the apologist is often regarded as an "aggressive, opportunistic person who tries, by fair means or foul, to argue people into joining the church."[1]

It's easy to see how these stereotypes arise. And it's equally easy to see how dangerous such attitudes can be. The heart of apologetics is not about mastering and memorizing a set of techniques designed to manipulate arguments to get the desired conclusion. It is about being mastered by the Christian faith so that its ideas, themes, and values are deeply imprinted on our minds and in our hearts.

Far from being a mechanical repetition of ideas, apologetics is about a natural realization of the answers we can provide to people's questions and concerns, answers that arise from a deep and passionate immersion in the realities of our faith. The best apologetics is done from the standpoint of the rich vision of reality characteristic of the Christian gospel, which gives rise to deeply realistic insights into human nature. What is our problem? What is our need? How can these needs be resolved? In each case, a powerful answer may be given to each question, an answer grounded in the Christian understanding of the nature of things.

As this book will emphasize, there is no substitute for long, hard, and prayerful reflection on the great truths of faith on the one hand, and the identity of the audiences we shall engage and address on the other. In this chapter, we shall consider how theological reflection on the central themes of the Christian faith informs good apologetics.

Setting Things in Context

To help us set our reflections in a proper context, let us recall one of the earliest recorded events in the Gospel accounts of the ministry of Jesus of Nazareth:

> As Jesus passed along the Sea of Galilee, he saw Simon and his brother Andrew casting a net into the sea—for they were fishermen. And Jesus said to them, "Follow me and I will make you fish for people." And immediately they left their nets and followed him. (Mark 1:16–18)

This is a wonderful narrative, packed full of detail and insight. For example, we note that Jesus called *fishermen*. Contemporary Jewish literature had much to say about people whose jobs made them virtually incapable of keeping the law of Moses. Two groups often singled out for special (negative) comment were carpenters and fishermen—carpenters because they doubled as undertakers and were handling dead bodies all the time, and fishermen because they had to handle and sort mixed catches of clean and unclean fish. Both groups were incapable of observing the strict Jewish rules about ritual purity, which prohibited contact with anything unclean. Yet Jesus calls precisely such fishermen, who hovered on the fringes of Jewish religious life. It's a powerful reminder of the way in which the Christian gospel reaches out to everyone—even those whom society regards as powerless or valueless.

That's an important point. But it's not the most important thing from an apologetic point of view. Here's the apologetic question we need to ask: What made Simon and Andrew leave everything and follow Jesus? Does Jesus offer compelling arguments for the existence of God? Does he explain to them that he is the fulfillment of the great prophecies of the Old Testament? No. There is something about him that is compelling. The response of Simon and Andrew was immediate and intuitive. Mark leaves us with the impression of an utterly compelling figure who commands assent by his very presence.

Although this account of the encounter between Jesus of Nazareth and the first disciples by the Sea of Galilee is very familiar, we need to read it with an apologetic agenda in mind. It helps us set apologetics in its proper perspective. It reminds us that argument can be only part of our strategy. In many ways, our task is to lead people to Christ and discovery of the living God. Apologetics does not and cannot convert anyone. But it can point people in the right direction by removing barriers to an encounter with God, or opening a window through which Christ can be seen. Apologetics is about enabling people to grasp the significance of the gospel. It is about pointing, explaining, opening doors, and removing barriers. Yet what converts is not apologetics itself, but the greater reality of God and the risen Christ.

To explain this important point, we may turn to another account of the calling of the first disciples:

> Philip found Nathanael and said to him, "We have found him about whom Moses in the law and also the prophets wrote, Jesus son of Joseph from Nazareth." Nathanael said to him, "Can anything good come out of Nazareth?" Philip said to him, "Come and see." (John 1:45–46)

Having encountered Jesus of Nazareth, Philip is convinced he is the one he has been hoping for. He then tries to persuade Nathanael that Jesus is the fulfillment of the hopes of Israel. Nathanael is clearly skeptical about this, and raises an objection: Could such a person really come from Nazareth? Yet instead of meeting this objection with reasoned argument, Philip invites Nathanael to meet Jesus of Nazareth and decide for himself.

Now Philip might have answered Nathanael with a detailed argument. Perhaps he might have argued that Jesus's origins in Nazareth represented the fulfillment of a biblical prophecy. Or perhaps he might have set out the various factors that led him, Andrew, and Peter to follow Jesus of Nazareth and believe him to be the culmination of the hopes of Israel. Yet Philip has learned that *encounter* is to be preferred to *argument*. Why argue with Nathanael when there is a more direct and appropriate way of resolving the matter? And so Philip says, "Come and see."

On meeting Jesus and hearing him, Nathanael comes to his own conclusion: "Rabbi, you are the Son of God! You are the King of Israel!" (John 1:49). We see here the importance of pointing people toward Jesus of Nazareth. We can, like Philip, explain what we find so powerfully compelling and attractive about Jesus. But in the end, the ultimate persuasion comes not from our testimony, but from one's own encounter with the risen Christ.

The point is important. Apologetics, we are often told, is about persuading people of the truth of the Christian faith. Now there is some truth in that—but it is not the whole truth. There are serious limits to the scope of arguments. You may be able to persuade someone that an idea is correct—but is this going to change his or her life? Philip rightly discerns that Nathanael will be transformed not by an argument, nor even an idea, but by a personal encounter with Jesus. He does not *argue for* Jesus—he *points to* Jesus. Is this not a helpful model for Christian witness—pointing people to Jesus, whom we have found to be the fulfillment of human longings and the culmination of our aspirations, thus allowing them to encounter him for themselves, rather than relying on our arguments and explanations?

Yet the story continues, and there are further apologetic points to be made. A few days later, Jesus and his disciples attend a wedding at Cana in Galilee. There, Jesus performs a "sign"—he changes water into wine. The impact of this sign on the disciples is significant. As the Gospel narrative tells us, "Jesus did this, the first of his signs, in Cana of Galilee, and revealed his glory; and his disciples believed in him" (John 2:11). Faith is here seen as the outcome of a revelation of the glory of Christ. This goes far beyond reasoned argument. Faith is the response to the realization of the full majesty, glory, and wonder of Christ. Perhaps the most striking example of this is "Doubting Thomas," who puts his faith in Christ when he realizes he has indeed been raised from the dead: "My Lord and my God!" (John 20:28).

Even this brief discussion of the nature of apologetics indicates that it has a strongly theological dimension. It may be helpful to explore this in a little more detail before proceeding further.

First, the references in John's Gospel to faith arising from the revelation of divine glory remind us that conversion is not brought about by human wisdom or reasoning, but is in its deepest sense something that is brought about by God. This is a constant theme in the New Testament. Paul's preaching at Corinth did not rest on human wisdom, "so that your faith might rest not on human wisdom but on the power of God" (1 Cor. 2:5). Faith is not about a mere change of mind; it is about personal transformation through an encounter with the living God.

Second, the New Testament depicts human nature as being wounded and damaged by sin. We are not capable of seeing things as they really are. "The god of this world has blinded the minds of the unbelievers, to keep them from seeing the light of the gospel of the glory of Christ, who is the image of God" (2 Cor. 4:4). Arguments do not cure blindness, nor does the accumulation of evidence, powerful rhetoric, or a compelling personal testimony. Blindness needs to be *healed*—and such a healing is something only God is able to do. God alone is able to open the eyes of the blind and enable them to see the realities of life. Apologetics thus depends upon the grace of God and the divine capacity to heal and renew. This is not something we can do. This helps put apologetics in proper perspective!

Third, this theological perspective sets the apologetic task in its proper context. We realize we have an important but limited role to play in bringing people to faith. God is the one who will convert; we have the privilege of bringing people to a point at which God takes over. We point to the source of healing; God heals. We witness to the power of forgiveness; God forgives. We explain how God has changed our lives, transforming them for the better; God enters lives, and changes them. We have a real and privileged part in this process, but are not left on our own. Apologetics is always undertaken in the power and presence of the risen Christ.

An analogy may help make this critically important point clearer. Imagine you had blood poisoning some years ago. Certain symptoms developed, and you realized you were seriously ill. A skilled physician told you what the problem was. And there was a cure: penicillin. The drug was quickly administered, and within days you were on the road to recovery. It's a very easy scenario to imagine, and you could rewrite it easily to widen its reach.

Here's the critical question: Did the physician heal you? In one sense, yes. In another, no. The physician told you what was wrong with you, and what needed to be done if you were to be healed. But what actually cured you was penicillin. The physician's diagnosis told you what the problem was. But in the days before penicillin was discovered, this condition meant only one thing: death. There was nothing that could be done to save you. Identifying the problem would not have been enough to heal you. A cure was needed.

This analogy allows us to get a good sense of how apologetics works, and how we fit into the greater scheme of things. To continue this medical analogy, apologetics is about explaining that human nature is wounded, damaged, broken, and fallen—and that it can be healed by God's grace. The apologist can use many strategies to explain, communicate, and defend the idea that there is something wrong with human nature. Equally, we can use many strategies to explain, communicate, and defend the fact that there is indeed a cure. But apologetics itself does not heal; it only points to where a cure may be found.

We may provide excellent arguments that such a cure exists. We could provide personal testimonies from people whose lives have been changed by discovering this cure. But in the end, people are healed only by finding and receiving the cure, and allowing it to do its work. We may play a real and important role in helping them to realize they are ill and telling them how they could be cured. Without us, they might not find the cure. But the actual process of healing itself results from the power of penicillin, not from our words.

Apologetics and a Theological Vision of Reality

Apologetics is grounded in a deep appreciation of the intellectual capaciousness and spiritual richness of the Christian faith. The task of the apologist is not to make the Christian faith attractive or relevant to the world. Rather, we are called on to help people appreciate and discover its power, relevance, and persuasiveness. The apologist is called on to work out how to allow the intrinsic truth, beauty, and goodness of the Christian faith to be discerned.

Another analogy might help clarify this point. Imagine you are standing on a mountain with a friend, admiring the view. It's a scene you know well, as you've been there many times before. But your friend hasn't. It's all new to her. Below you, the landscape stretches into the far distance. You can see forests, rivers, fields, and villages. You point out the villages, telling your friend about their histories. You show her the rivers, and tell her about the ancient forests. You point out a little waterfall that is easy to miss unless you know what to look for. She is delighted with the scene. But the point to appreciate is that you did not create its beauty or its history. You merely helped her to appreciate what was already there—something she didn't know about, or hadn't noticed.

Apologetics is not about inventing the rationality, imaginative power, or moral depths of the Christian faith. It is about pointing them out, and allowing people to see them clearly and appreciate them for what they are. This means the apologist must be able and willing to develop a deep and informed appreciation of the Christian faith. Yet this is not enough: it is also important to develop an outsider perspective. We need to be able to understand how the great themes of the Christian faith can be defended and explained to people who are not familiar with its vocabulary or practices. Perhaps even more importantly, we need to be able to work out how these themes relate to people, so they can begin to appreciate their relevance and power of transformation.

So, how can we appreciate the power and depth of the Christian faith through theological analysis? We begin by considering an analogy that many have found helpful in appreciating the importance of theology in apologetics. I first began to use this analogy in the late 1980s, and have been encouraged by how many people have adopted it (and sometimes adapted it as well!). The analogy? A prism.

In 1666, the great British mathematician and physicist Isaac Newton made a discovery in his rooms at Trinity College, Cambridge. If a beam of white light were passed through a glass prism, it was broken up into the seven colors of the rainbow—red, orange, yellow, green, blue, indigo, and violet.[2] Newton realized that a similar process must lie behind the formation of the colors of the rainbow, with raindrops breaking down the white light of the sun into its constituent colors. Each color was already present in the beam of white light, but its individual identity was not obvious. The prism allowed the colors to be separated so that each could be seen and appreciated.

It's a simple analogy, but it allows us to make a powerful point. The Christian gospel—like a beam of white light—is a rich, complex reality, consisting of a number of elements. Each of these elements deserves to be studied and appreciated in its own right. Theological analysis is about identifying each of these elements of Christian proclamation, determining its apologetic potential, and using it appropriately.

To make this point clearer, we shall undertake a piece of theological analysis and use this apologetically. Let's ask a simple question: What is the significance of the cross of Christ? Although this is an important theological question, it is equally important apologetically. Different people have different needs and concerns. One aspect of the gospel may interlock with one group of needs, while another may match up with others.

A Worked Example: Theological Analysis of the Cross

It is impossible to summarize the immensely rich and complex message of the cross in a few words. Indeed, one of the great delights of theology is that it offers us the opportunity of reflecting deeply (and at leisure!) on the full meaning of the great themes of the Christian message, such as the cross of Christ.[3] Yet it is important to note that a number of aspects can be identified within that message—each of which has particular relevance to certain groups of people. Each aspect of the Christian proclamation of the cross of Christ will resonate particularly with specific groups of people outside the church.

For our purposes in this section, we shall consider four leading themes associated with the cross of Christ. All four play an important

role in the New Testament witness to the significance of the death
of Christ and subsequent reflection on the extended meaning of this
event within the Christian theological tradition.

1. The cross of Christ is the basis of the forgiveness of human sin.
2. The cross and resurrection of Christ achieve victory over sin
   and death.
3. The cross brings healing to broken and wounded humanity.
4. The cross demonstrates the love of God for humanity.

Other themes could easily be added to this short list. My intention here is not to provide an exhaustive theological analysis of the
cross, but to show how identification of its themes has significant
and important apologetic applications. I shall elaborate briefly on
each of these four theological points before exploring their apologetic implications.

1. The cross of Christ is the basis of the forgiveness of human sin.

A good starting point for our reflection is Paul's declaration that
"Christ died for our sins" (1 Cor. 15:3). It is not just the brute and
crude historical fact of the death of Christ that is of such importance; it is what that event means for us. That Jesus died is history;
that Jesus died *for the forgiveness of our sins* is the gospel. For Paul,
the cross meant salvation, forgiveness, and victory over death. Thus
the "message of the cross" is not restricted to the simple fact that
Jesus was crucified, but extends to the significance of this event for
us. Jesus died—in order that we might live. Jesus was numbered
among sinners so that sinners might be forgiven.

Much more could be said about the theology of forgiveness. This
book, however, is about apologetics, not theology. Our concern here
is to focus on outsider perspectives. How does the proclamation of
the possibility of real forgiveness of real sins through the death of
Christ relate to people outside the Christian faith? How can this
theological truth interlock with their anxieties and aspirations? We
need to learn to think apologetically, reflecting on how this aspect
of the cross might be a gateway for someone to discover the reality

of the gospel. How might we use this idea of forgiveness as a bridge to God?

One way of beginning to make these connections focuses on the question of human guilt—a deep concern for many. Philosopher Immanuel Kant commented that a deep sense of guilt holds many people back from moral action. While there is some truth in this, there is a much deeper point that needs to be made. Some people have such a deep sense of guilt about something they have done—or, in some cases, have had done to them—that they feel they cannot really live properly until the problem has been resolved. How, they wonder, can they achieve this?

This, of course, is a central theme in one of the best-known works of English literature—John Bunyan's classic *The Pilgrim's Progress*. Bunyan depicts his pilgrim as struggling under a "burden of sin" that forces him to his knees, making him unable to walk properly. Finally, he is able to lay this burden at the foot of the cross and begin to walk properly for the first time. That is how many people feel: they are burdened with guilt, and realize they cannot begin to live properly until they know they have been properly forgiven.

The word "sin," of course, is problematic for many today. We must avoid thinking that this is a recent development. Back in 1945, C. S. Lewis complained that "a sense of sin is almost totally lacking" in modern culture. The apologist must deal with "people who have been raised to believe that whatever goes wrong in the world is someone else's fault."[4] Sin—like every aspect of the apologist's vocabulary—needs to be explained.[5]

2. The cross and resurrection of Christ achieve victory over sin and death.

One great theme of the gospel is that the cross and resurrection of Jesus Christ free us from the fear of death. Christ has been raised from the dead, and those who have faith will one day share in that resurrection and be with him forever. Death is no longer something we need to fear. Christians celebrate this supremely at Easter, when they recall with gratitude the costliness of this victory and exult in its reality. This great message of hope in the face of suffering and death is crucial for us all. Yet it has a special relevance to those many people who wake up in the middle of the night, frightened by the thought of death. Many people in western culture are simply unable or unwilling to confront the reality of human mortality. They hope they can get through life without having to deal with it. But you can't run away from reality. You've got to face up to the way things really are.

A classic study of the western reluctance to face the reality of human mortality is found in Ernest Becker's prize-winning study *The Denial of Death*. Becker argues that many westerners maintain a pretense of immortality, refusing to concede their own mortality. It is too difficult and too painful a matter to think about. It is therefore sidelined and ignored—but it won't just go away.

The cross liberates us from the fear of death and the need to live a lie. It acts as a powerful antidote to our natural tendency to be frightened or anxious about our situation in the world. It allows us to face death with a quiet and calm confidence, knowing that its sting has been drawn by the cross and victory given through the resurrection. The letter to the Hebrews makes this point powerfully when it declares Jesus died in order that he might "destroy the one who has the power of death, that is, the devil, and free those who all their lives were held in slavery by the fear of death" (Heb. 2:14–15).

Now notice this approach isn't saying, "Let's pretend death has been defeated. Let's pretend its power has been broken. And let's live our lives as if death should not worry us." That would be like closing our eyes to the harsh realities of life and living in a make-believe world of fantasy—like stepping into a fairy tale, or into an arcade game of Dungeons & Dragons. No! This approach is saying something very different indeed. It is saying, "Through the cross and resurrection of Jesus Christ, the power of death has been broken. We have been given victory over death through Christ. And that knowledge ought to change us. It ought to transform the way we think and the way we live. We need not fear death anymore, because on the cross Christ grappled with it, and defeated it." This is no pretend world of an overexcited and fertile human imagination. It is the real world of the gospel, given and guaranteed by God himself.

The apologetic implications of this are momentous, especially for those who know the fear of death and want to break free from its thrall. Many have failed to come to life because they are so frightened of death. The Christian gospel meets these concerns head-on. There is no need to run away from reality anymore.

3. The cross brings healing to broken and wounded humanity.

One of the central themes of the Christian Scriptures is that God heals a broken world and restores damaged people. The prophets emphasized this hope of healing, comparing God to a physician or to a "sun of righteousness [that] shall rise, with healing in its wings" (Mal. 4:2). Jesus of Nazareth's healing ministry can be seen as an extension of this theme, pointing to God's renewal of his creation through his agency.

This theme is intensified through a focus on the cross, which the New Testament sees as a fulfillment of the "suffering servant" theme of the prophecy of Isaiah:

> Surely he has borne our infirmities and carried our diseases; yet we accounted him stricken, struck down by God, and afflicted. But he was wounded for our transgressions, crushed for our iniquities; upon him was the punishment that made us whole, and by his bruises we are healed. (Isa. 53:4–5)

The crucified Christ's wounds and suffering are thus seen in a deeper light. In some way, Christ bore this pain and suffering for others, in order that they might be healed.

Early Christian writers were aware of the apologetic importance of this theme. In the late first century, Ignatius of Antioch spoke of the "medicine of immortality"—in other words, comparing the gospel to a drug able to heal humanity's fatal illness, so that death need no longer be feared. In the fifth century, Augustine of Hippo suggested the church was like a hospital—full of wounded and ill people who were recovering under the care of the good physician and the medicine he provided. The same theme is taken up, powerfully and memorably, in a great African American spiritual:

> There is balm in Gilead,
> To make the wounded whole;
> There's power enough in heaven,
> To cure a sin-sick soul.

So how can this theme be used apologetically? How does it speak to the cultural mood and to the aspirations and concerns of ordinary people? Many people think of society as broken, or of themselves as damaged or wounded. This is a powerful and meaningful way of expressing a deep feeling that things are not right. Things need to be restored to what they were meant to be. But where is healing to be found?

At this point, a powerful connection can be established with the Christian faith. This can be developed *iconically*—in other words, through images. The familiar image of a wounded, suffering Christ on the cross, when rightly interpreted, speaks of God's solidarity with those suffering and the possibility of renewal and restoration. It can also be developed *intellectually*, in terms of Christ entering into the vale of human sorrow and pain in order to transform it. It is no accident that the great New Testament vision of the New Jerusalem emphasizes that sorrow and pain have been left behind. They will not be part of the new order. God "will wipe every tear from their eyes. Death will be no more; mourning and crying and pain will be no more, for the first things have passed away" (Rev. 21:4).

4. The cross demonstrates the love of God for humanity.

At the heart of the Christian faith lies belief in a trustworthy God who loves us. More than that: God demonstrates that love for humanity in and through the death of Christ on the cross. "God proves his love for us in that while we still were sinners Christ died for us" (Rom. 5:8). The full extent of this love is revealed in the cross of Christ. Jesus died in order to convince and assure us of the tender love of God for us sinners (John 3:16), and thus to bring us home to God. Some people feel they are too deeply immersed in their sin to be loved by God; the New Testament takes a very different view, affirming that nothing can separate us from the love of God in Christ (Rom. 8:31–39).

The Christian faith declares that the love of God is revealed and confirmed in action. It is certainly true that "God is love" (1 John 4:8). Yet this could easily be misunderstood as some timeless truth that affirms God as the true ideal of *human* love. That is inadequate

as a description of the Christian God. The Bible witnesses to a
God who, like the shepherd who has lost a sheep, goes out in search
of it and carries it home rejoicing (Luke 15:4–7). We see this supremely demonstrated in the cross of Christ, in which God acted
to demonstrate this love. "God's love was revealed among us in this
way: God sent his only Son into the world so that we might live
through him" (1 John 4:9). Actions, as we are continually reminded,
speak louder than words. God is dynamic, a living God, an *acting*
God, who does things in order to reveal the full extent of his love
for us.

So how can this important theological insight be used apologetically? How does it speak to where our culture is at the moment?
Everyone wants to matter. We all need a "secure base"—a context
within which we are loved, affirmed, and enabled to grow and develop. Families, friends, and communities alike have the potential
to offer support. Yet many people often feel lonely and lost along
the road of life, overwhelmed by thoughts of the vastness of the
universe and the brevity and insignificance of human life. Who
cares about us?

The theme of the love of God speaks of a God who is present and
who cares. We matter profoundly to him. God knows us individually by name. As the psalmist declares, contemplating the vastness
of the starry heavens:

> When I look at your heavens, the work of your fingers,
>   the moon and the stars that you have established;
> What are human beings that you are mindful of them,
>   mortals that you care for them?
> Yet you have made them a little lower than God,
>   and crowned them with glory and honor. (Ps. 8:3–5)

This powerful affirmation is deepened and strengthened through
the message of the cross of Christ, which speaks of the God who
created all things *entering into* his creation in order to redeem us. So
"mindful" is God of each of us that Christ chose to die for each of
us. He gave all that he had for us. As C. S. Lewis remarked, Christians do not think "God will love us because we are good, but that
God will make us good because he loves us."[6]

Moving On

In this chapter, we have seen how theological reflection on core themes and elements of the Christian gospel allow us to begin to make connections with audiences. The same type of thinking can be applied again and again. The important thing is to bring the gospel into contact with people's lives. Theology helps us identify the most appropriate point of contact with individuals, so that they can discover the joy of faith. This doesn't mean we are reducing the gospel to just one point! It means we are looking for the aspect of the gospel that is of greatest relevance to the person we are talking to. The rest of the gospel will follow in due course. We have to start somewhere with each specific audience—and theology helps identify the best starting point in each case.

In the next chapter, we shall focus more closely on the identity of the audience. How does this impact the way we do apologetics?

For Further Reading

Allen, Diogenes. *Christian Belief in a Postmodern World: The Full Wealth of Conviction*. Louisville: Westminster John Knox, 1989.

Grenz, Stanley J., and William C. Placher. *Essentials of Christian Theology*. Louisville: Westminster John Knox, 2003.

McGrath, Alister E. *Christian Theology: An Introduction*, 5th ed. Oxford: Wiley-Blackwell, 2011.

Sire, James W. *A Little Primer on Humble Apologetics*. Downers Grove, IL: InterVarsity, 2006.

Sproul, R. C. *Defending Your Faith: An Introduction to Apologetics*. Wheaton: Crossway, 2003.

4

The Importance of
the Audience

POSSIBILITIES AND ISSUES

We need to ensure the message of the cross is proclaimed as effectively as possible. This means asking what points of contact there are for the gospel. How can we make sure it scratches where folks itch? To lapse into jargon for a moment, the gospel proclamation must be *receptor-oriented*; that is, it must be addressed to the opportunities that await it among its audience. Just as the science of apologetics is partly concerned with the theological analysis of the Christian proclamation, so the art of apologetics is concerned with the imaginative and creative application of its respective components to its audiences.

So how might the identity of any audience shape our apologetic approach? After all, surely we are trying to present the same gospel to everyone, yes? Why not use a single presentation of the nature and significance of the gospel? It would make the apologist's task a lot simpler. Yet a little more reflection makes it clear that we cannot adopt such a simplistic approach. As we shall see, the New Testament itself develops a variety of apologetic arguments and styles of engagement, clearly intended to facilitate connection with each specific envisaged audience.

Consider Paul's use of the image of adoption as a powerful visual image of redemption.[1] Paul clearly uses this image in his letters in the expectation that his readers will be familiar with it and understand how it illuminates the consequences of Christ's death and resurrection. Yet the concept of adoption was neither known to, nor permitted by, Jewish law. It was a legal category familiar to people throughout the Greco-Roman world. Unsurprisingly, Paul uses this image in letters written to churches in Rome and other regions in the Greco-Roman world—such as the city of Ephesus and the region of Galatia.[2] No New Testament writer uses this image when writing to a Jewish readership.

Most evangelical apologists rightly base their apologetic strategies on the writings of Paul, especially his letter to the Romans. Yet Paul's letters are written to *Christians*—that is, to people who already believe, and who need instruction, encouragement, and guidance. They are not addressed to interested unbelievers or inquirers. It is certainly true that Paul has the interests of such people at heart, and at several points in his letters it is clear he is concerned about the negative impression the behavior of certain Christians may create for such people. For example, 1 Corinthians clearly expresses anxieties about what interested unbelievers will think about the gospel if they judge it on the basis of what was rumored to happen in public worship at Corinth!

The two sections of the New Testament that presuppose their audiences are interested unbelievers are the Gospels and the Acts of the Apostles. The Gospels record encounters between Jesus and individuals that are clearly of value to us as we work out how to best present the person and work of Jesus Christ to our own culture. But my particular interest in this chapter concerns the Acts of the Apostles, which records a series of addresses and apologetic approaches adopted by Paul and other prominent early Christians, especially Peter. Here, we find material that is explicitly apologetic in nature. In a series of addresses and incidents, we find Paul and others directly engaging with the ideas and concerns of a number of major social groups. As the narrative of Acts (and, indeed, the history of the early church) makes clear, each of these groups came to be represented in the early church, and to play an important role in its outreach.

These early apologetic approaches in Acts offer us important insights into authentically biblical methods of apologetics, as well as suggesting strategies for engaging with specific groups of major importance to the development of the early church. We will explore the broad apologetic strategies developed by Peter and Paul in key speeches in Acts, in which they engage directly with the concerns of three significant groups of people: the Jews, the Greeks, and the Romans. In each case, the concerns and approaches are different—yet the same gospel is defended on each occasion. It is conveyed and affirmed in different manners, resting on reflection about the most appropriate manner of bringing the good news of Jesus Christ to each specific group. Let's begin by exploring the defense and commendation of the gospel to the Jewish people set out in Peter's famous Pentecost sermon of Acts 2.

Apologetics to the Jews: Peter's Pentecost Speech (Acts 2)

Christianity has its origins within Judaism. It is clear that a major issue faced by early Christian writers was the question of the relationship between Christianity and Judaism. In what ways did Jesus Christ relate to Israel? To what extent was there continuity and discontinuity between God's dealings with the Jewish people and the new dispensation inaugurated through the life, death, and resurrection of Jesus Christ?

Christians themselves have always been clear that Christianity is continuous with Judaism. The "God of Abraham, Isaac, and Jacob" is the same as the "God of Jesus Christ." Early Christianity emerged within Judaism, and most of the first converts to the movement were Jews. The New Testament frequently mentions Christians preaching in local synagogues. So similar were the two movements that outside observers such as the Roman authorities tended to treat Christianity as a sect within Judaism rather than as a new movement with a distinct identity. So how could the gospel be explained to Jews? It is clear that one central issue concerned the identity of Jesus, particularly his status in relation to the people of Israel.

The major text to be analyzed here is Peter's famous sermon, preached on the Day of Pentecost (Acts 2:14–40).[3] Luke—who is widely believed to have written both the Gospel known by his name and the book of Acts—is absolutely clear about the identity of the audience to which Peter preached. They were "devout Jews from every nation under heaven living in Jerusalem" (Acts 2:5). The theme dominating this sermon is that the coming of Jesus—or, to be more precise, the entire economy of salvation, including the resurrection of Jesus of Nazareth and the giving of the Holy Spirit—fulfills Old Testament prophecy. The basic structure of the address is as follows:

> Section 1 (2:14–21): Setting the events of the Day of Pentecost in the light of Old Testament prophecy. The remarkable events that unfolded before the eyes of this Jewish audience can only be understood in the light of God's promises to his people in the Old Testament—promises that have now been fulfilled.
>
> Section 2 (2:22–28): The affirmation of the exaltation of Jesus of Nazareth in the light of Old Testament expectations. Once more, the continuity between the Old Testament and the coming of Jesus is demonstrated. The consistent appeal to prophecy, which would have been devoid of significance to a Gentile audience, would have been of the greatest importance to pious Jews.
>
> Section 3 (2:29–36): The affirmation of the exaltation of Jesus of Nazareth, along with the theological interpretation of this: "This Jesus whom you crucified" has been made "both Lord and Messiah."
>
> Section 4 (2:37–40): A call to repentance in order to benefit from the salvation that results.

The first point to note is the way in which Peter's apologetic is directly related to themes that were important and comprehensible to a Jewish audience. The expectation of the coming of the Messiah was (and still remains!) significant for Judaism. Peter here makes three very significant apologetic moves. First, he demonstrates that Jesus meets the specific expectations of Israel. Second, he appeals to specific authorities (here, prophetic passages in the Old Testament) that carry weight with his audience. And third, he uses language and terminology readily accepted and understood by his audience. Note in particular his specific reference to Jesus as "Lord and Messiah." No explanation of these two technical terms is offered, or necessary.

Both ideas were familiar to his audience, and both *mattered* to his audience. What was new about Peter's message was his emphatic insistence that the resurrection of Christ was the basis of recognizing him as both Lord and Messiah.

The importance of interpretation in apologetics needs to be highlighted here. Peter does not merely *assert* the historical actuality of the death and resurrection of Jesus; he offers a specific *interpretation* of them. An appeal to history is a vital and distinct function in the armory of the Christian apologist. It reassures insiders of the reliability of the Gospel accounts of the great historical events upon which faith rests.

But what of outsiders? What role does an appeal to historical evidence have to someone outside the faith? Will it enable them to come to faith? An appeal to the evidence of history unquestionably has an important role to play here. It minimizes a significant obstacle to faith—the criticism, often made by atheist writers, that the New Testament is "made up," lacking any real historical roots. It poses a powerful challenge to those who argue, usually on rather flimsy grounds, that Christianity is just some kind of wish-fulfillment, by stressing the historical events that brought Christianity into being. Christian faith arose in part as a response to the history of Jesus of Nazareth.

Yet historical apologetics is vulnerable. It details events; the gospel concerns an *interpretation* of events. Historical apologetics asks, "Did this really happen?" Yet the big questions of life concern the meaning of events, not just the events themselves. Indeed, it is fair to suggest it is their *perceived significance* that gives historical duration to events.

It's an important point, and needs to be considered further. To help us appreciate the issues, consider a critical moment in the career of the famous Roman soldier and statesman Julius Caesar. In 49 BC, Caesar led an army south from Gaul (modern-day France) into Italy. At one point, they had to cross a river—the Rubicon. Contemporary reports suggest it was not a particularly wide or deep river. Crossing it posed no particular physical difficulties. The act of crossing the Rubicon, in itself, was thus of no real historical significance.

Yet the Rubicon was a political marker, defining the northern frontier of the territory governed directly by the Roman senate. Crossing this international boundary line without permission and with an army, therefore, amounted to a declaration of war by Caesar against Rome. The crossing of the Rubicon is important because it marked the beginning of one of the most famous civil wars in history. Yet only an observer familiar with the situation at the time would realize the full implications of what Caesar had done; an untrained observer would simply have noticed an army crossing a rather unimportant river. People cross rivers every day of the week. There is nothing special about even armies crossing a river—such maneuvers are, after all, the staple diet of military training. But the crossing of this specific river, at this specific time in history, represented a declaration of war.

We need therefore to establish not just what happened, but how the event should be interpreted. We must ascertain the context that gives the event its meaning. The principle is the same whether we are dealing with Caesar crossing the Rubicon or Jesus of Nazareth dying on the cross and rising again from the dead. The historical significance of the event needs to be settled. It is this process that can be seen at work in the New Testament, especially the writings of Paul. It is at this point that purely historical apologetics, dedicated to establishing what happened, begins to falter. Events need to be supplemented with interpretation. As Paul put it in his letter to the Romans, Christ "was handed over to death for our trespasses and was raised for our justification" (Rom. 4:25). Note how Paul seamlessly merges historical affirmation (Christ was handed over to death and was raised from the dead) with theological interpretation (these things happened to bring about our forgiveness and justification).

So what is the significance of Peter's sermon for us today? It reminds us of the compelling case that can be made for Jesus representing the culmination of God's dealings with his chosen people. As Peter insists, the resurrection of Jesus is the culmination of the many clues leading to the conclusion that he is "Lord and Messiah." Good apologetics is not just about the affirmation of historical facts. We are not out to prove simply that Jesus died on a cross and rose again. We want to convey the significance of those facts for a fallen and lost world.

Nor is good apologetics merely about the affirmation of spiritual insights—for example, the ability of the Christian faith to meet the deepest needs of humanity. These insights are given in and through historical events. Once these events are rightly understood, their deep spiritual meaning can be grasped. The event and its meaning are thus given together, and need to be proclaimed together. Peter's Pentecost sermon gives us some vital clues about how best to do this.

Apologetics to the Greeks: Paul's Athens Sermon (Acts 17)

One of the most important audiences envisaged by New Testament writers for proclamation of the gospel is "the Greeks." In Paul's first letter to the Corinthians, "Greeks" are set alongside "Jews" as a defining group of considerable importance (1 Cor. 1:22). It is quite clear that sections of the Acts of the Apostles show at least some degree of familiarity and affinity with Hellenistic rhetoric, as well as the beliefs and practices of the classical period.[4]

One of the most important early engagements between Christianity and these classic philosophical beliefs is found in Paul's address in the Greek city of Athens, the site of the Platonic Academy. Although Athens had been a major political and cultural center in the classical period under Pericles, it had entered into a period of decline by the time of Paul's visit. Athens had become little more than a provincial city within the Roman empire, having lost much of its former glory and importance. Greece suffered a serious setback when it was unwise enough to back the losing side in the Roman civil war. Nevertheless, Athens retained iconic significance, even if the reality no longer quite matched up to the image it sought to project. If Christianity was to take root in this city, it would have to engage the city's formidable philosophical heritage. Paul stepped up to the plate, and rose to this challenge.

According to Luke, Paul opens his address to the Athenians with a gradual introduction of the theme of the living God, allowing the religious and philosophical curiosity of the Athenians to shape the contours of his theological exposition.[5] He makes an appeal to a "sense of divinity" present in each individual as a point of contact for the Christian faith. By doing this, Paul connects with existing Greek theistic assumptions, while at the same time demonstrating how the Christian gospel goes beyond them. Paul shows a clear appreciation of the apologetic potential of Stoic philosophy, portraying the gospel as resonating with central Stoic concerns, while extending the limits of what might be known. What the Greeks held to be unknown, possibly unknowable, Paul proclaims to have been made known through the resurrection of Christ. Paul is able to relate with the experiential and cognitive world of his audience—without compromising the integrity of the Christian faith.

So what authorities does Paul use to connect with his Athenian audience? It is important to appreciate here that the Athenians knew nothing of the Old Testament. Whereas Peter's Pentecost sermon is addressed to a Jewish audience deeply steeped in a knowledge of the Old Testament, Paul's Athens sermon engages people from a very different cultural context. Paul finds himself in a situation in which he must proclaim the gospel without being able to make connections with the history and hopes of Israel. So how does he do this?

Where Peter appeals to the "book of Scripture," Paul turns instead to the "book of nature." It is an idea with roots deeply embedded in Scripture: "The heavens are telling the glory of God; and the firmament proclaims his handiwork" (Ps. 19:1). Paul believed passionately in the theological truth and apologetic importance of this insight (see especially Rom. 1–2). An appeal to God as creator thus becomes a channel for introducing the theme of redemption in Christ.

Paul is clearly aware of the distinct identity and characteristics of his audience, and uses local beliefs and landmarks as anchors for his apologetic presentation. Since his audience does not know the Old Testament, Paul draws upon literary authorities with which they are familiar—in this case, the Athenian poet Aratus, widely regarded as one of the great cultural icons of his day. Aratus dates from the late fourth and early third centuries before Christ, and it is thought that his place of birth was Soli in Paul's own province of Cilicia. Aratus studied Stoic philosophy in Athens at the school founded by Zeno. Little remains of his literary output today. Yet it is clear why Paul chose to cite from him in this way:

> [God] is not far from each one of us. For "In him we live and move and have our being"; as even some of your own poets have said, "For we too are his offspring." (Acts 17:27–28)

Paul here quotes a half-line from Aratus to reinforce—not to establish—his own point about God being close to hand.

A second local landmark also plays a key role in Paul's approach—the inscription on an altar that reads "To an unknown god" (Acts 17:23). The literature of the age, such as the writings of Diogenes Laertius, refer to such "anonymous altars" around this time. Paul here argues that a god of whom the Greeks had some implicit or intuitive awareness is now being made known to them by name and in full in the gospel. The God who is known indirectly through the created order can be known fully through the resurrection of Jesus Christ.

Paul's apologetic address at Athens offers important insights about how to adapt the proclamation of the gospel to a local audience. Peter's approach to a Jewish audience in Jerusalem would not have connected with Paul's audience in Athens, any more than Paul's approach in Athens would have resonated well with Peter's audience in Jerusalem. Paul adapts his rhetoric to the local situation, citing a local authority (the poet Aratus), exploiting the apologetic potential of a local landmark (an anonymous altar), and developing a line of thought that chimed in with some Athenian ideas about the presence of the divine in the natural order. It's an approach that can easily be adopted and adapted today.

Apologetics to the Romans: Paul's Legal Speeches (Acts 24–26)

The third audience early Christianity encountered was the Romans. At that time, Rome was the imperial force dominating the Mediterranean world. It is clear that the imperial Roman authorities regarded the emergence of Christianity with suspicion. One reason for this was its potential to create trouble in a socially volatile region of the empire. Yet there was another, perhaps more significant reason for this anxiety about Christianity—the so-called imperial cult.

The imperial cult was a form of civil religion based on a highly elevated view of the Roman emperor.[6] It emerged during the Augustan age, and appears to have become especially significant in the decades immediately preceding the birth of Christ. By AD 50—when Christianity was becoming a significant presence in the eastern regions of the Roman empire—the imperial cult had become firmly established as a routine aspect of Roman colonial life, especially in the eastern Mediterranean colonies. Worship of the Roman emperor was seen as an important means of ensuring social cohesion and stability throughout the empire. A refusal to take part in the imperial cult was seen as tantamount to political subversion or rebellion. Christians were vulnerable to charges of sedition if they refused to conform to these imperial cults.

Paul was accused of precisely such sedition at one point in his career. Charges were brought against him by the professional orator Tertullus (Acts 24:1–8). According to Tertullus, Paul was "an agitator among all the Jews throughout the world, and a ringleader of the sect of the Nazarene" (Acts 24:5). This was a serious charge, amounting to an accusation of political subversion and insurrection against the imperial Roman authorities. Paul needed to respond to these charges effectively and persuasively. The Greek word *apologia*—from which we get our term "apologetics"—often bears the sense of "a legal defense." This is precisely what we find Paul offering.

The most important speeches in Acts dealing with Christianity in the eyes of the Roman authorities are found in Acts 24–26. Recent studies have stressed the way in which these speeches conform to patterns that were well known in the legal proceedings of the period.[7] More than 250 papyri of official court proceedings in the early Roman empire exist, and they offer important insights into the way forensic proceedings were conducted and the manner in which they were recorded. In general terms, forensic speeches— whether offered by the prosecution or defense—tended to consist of four or five standard components. In the case of a speech for the defense, this would include a refutation of the specific charges brought against the accused.

The importance of this point can be seen by examining Paul's defense speech in Acts 24:10–21, in which he responds to the charges brought against him by Tertullus. It is important to note the way in which Paul follows—in the view of many scholars, with great skill—the "rules of engagement" laid down by Roman legal custom as he subjects Tertullus's accusations to a point-by-point refutation. In particular, Paul stresses the continuity between his own beliefs and those of the Jews who had accused him, particularly in regard to the Scriptures and the resurrection. But most significant is his appeal to Roman rules of evidence, which he deploys skillfully to outmaneuver his opponents.

Our concern in this discussion is not so much understanding what is happening in this important historical confrontation, but identifying its relevance to our apologetic situation today. The fine points of Roman legal arguments are not our concern here. The point is that Paul knew how Roman courts assessed evidence and was able to work with the grain of the system. Two points emerge with particular clarity.

First, it is important to note how Paul makes highly effective use of the "rules of engagement" of the Roman legal system. He grasps the importance of certain arguments in the eyes of those who would make the critical decisions concerning his future. And knowing what really matters, he is able to deliver the most effective defense of himself as a believer and of the Christian gospel. This point remains important today. We have to defend the gospel against its many critics. Yet we cannot simply treat all those who dislike or reject Christianity as being one homogeneous group. The reasons for rejecting Christianity vary, as do the reasons for accepting it. What may seem to be a highly persuasive argument for Christianity to one group of people may be an equally effective argument against it for another! We need to know the arguments that will carry weight with our audience.

Second, it is quite clear that both Paul and the Christian gospel were being misrepresented by his accusers and their legal representatives. Paul's general apologetic strategy is to set out clearly what he believes. A rejection of Christianity—whether this takes the form of a deliberate decision to have nothing to do with it or an unconscious sense of hostility toward it—depends on a prior understanding of what Christianity actually is. There is every possibility that a caricature or distortion has been rejected and the real thing has never been encountered or understood. For Paul, one of the best defenses of the Christian faith is its explanation.

Apologetics and Audiences: General Principles

As we have seen, it is very important to understand the different audiences we engage. Each has its own distinct identity, reflected in the particular concerns or difficulties it may experience concerning the Christian faith and the gateways that may be used to connect with it.

Three general principles emerge from our reflections on the apologetic addresses of the Acts of the Apostles. It may be helpful to summarize these points, and consider how we can make use of them today:

1. *Address the specific audience.* The three speeches explored here have very different audiences in mind. For example, Peter addresses Jews deeply versed in the Old Testament, and is aware of the hopes of Judaism; at Athens, Paul addresses the interests of secular Greek paganism, using terms it could understand. In each case, the apologetic approach is tailored to the particularities of that audience. We need to show that same ability (and take the trouble) to relate the unchanging gospel according to the very differing needs of the groups to whom we will speak.

2. Our second point is related to this. *Identify the authorities that carry weight with the audience.* Peter makes an appeal to the Old Testament, knowing it will be regarded as authoritative by his Jewish audience; Paul appeals to Greek poets as he seeks to defend the gospel in Athens. The apologist needs to work out what authorities carry weight with each audience, bearing in mind that an authority that carries a lot of weight with one audience may be regarded with disdain by another.

3. Finally, note that it is important to *use lines of argument that will carry weight with the audience.* Paul's careful conformity to Roman legal practice is an example of the general principle of trying to ensure the truth of the gospel is presented in the most effective manner for each audience we address. Paul's evidence for his innocence was secure and robust. But if it was presented in a way that did not conform to the expectations and conventions of his audience, it would seem weak and inadequate. Wisely, Paul chose to work within the conventional Roman framework for presenting evidence and developing arguments.

Apologetics and Audiences: Specific Issues

So how do we develop these points today? Their historical importance and biblical warrant is obvious. But how can we incorporate these ideas into our apologetic conversations, addresses, and writings? It is at this point the importance of apologetics as an *art* becomes obvious. The wise application of these principles demands imagination and flair as much as a good understanding of the situation.

The real issue concerns identifying the gateway that works best for our audiences. For some, that gateway will be evidence-based reasoning. Apologists have long recognized the importance of demonstrating the reasonableness of faith, and this remains an important task for contemporary apologetics. Other audiences, however, will use different criteria. Some will not see the question of the truth of the gospel as being of primary importance. For them, the question is whether it *works*. When engaging a pragmatic audience, the apologist will need to emphasize the difference the Christian faith makes in life. Other audiences will see morality as a key issue: Will the gospel help me work out what the good life looks like, and help me live it?

It is interesting to note that C. S. Lewis develops three quite different apologetic strategies in his writings, each of which relates to a distinct audience. In *Mere Christianity* (1952) and *Miracles* (1947), we find Lewis developing the case for the Christian faith based on an appeal to reason. The dominant apologetic theme in *The Pilgrim's Regress* (1933) and *Surprised by Joy* (1955) is that the Christian faith is the fulfillment of human longing. In the celebrated Narnia novels (1950–56), Lewis appeals to the imagination as the gateway to the human soul.

There is no inconsistency here; Lewis is simply identifying different elements of the Christian faith and deploying them apologetically—the approach we outlined in the previous chapter. Lewis rightly appreciated that each of these approaches would connect with different groups of people, and each needed a slightly different style of writing to enable these points to be communicated.

Moving On

In this chapter, we have considered the importance of the audience in shaping and informing apologetic approaches. In concluding, we noted how there are many gateways to faith—such as through beauty, imagination, or a longing for justice. We shall consider many of these approaches in a later chapter. Our attention first turns to one of the great themes of classical apologetics, which remains as important today as ever—namely, the claim that Christianity makes sense of things.

For Further Reading

Clark, David K. *Dialogical Apologetics: A Person-Centered Approach to Christian Defense*. Grand Rapids: Baker, 1993.

Heim, S. Mark. *The Depth of the Riches: A Trinitarian Theology of Religious Ends*. Grand Rapids: Eerdmans, 2001.

Placher, William C. *Unapologetic Theology: A Christian Voice in a Pluralistic Conversation*. Louisville: Westminster John Knox, 1989.

Stackhouse, John G. *Humble Apologetics: Defending the Faith Today*. Oxford: Oxford University Press, 2002.

5

The Reasonableness
of the Christian Faith

*A*pologetics is about persuading people that Christianity makes sense. C. S. Lewis, perhaps the greatest Christian apologist of the twentieth century, describes the capacity the Christian faith has to make sense of things with characteristic eloquence and concision: "I believe in Christianity as I believe that the sun has risen, not only because I see it, but because by it I see everything else."[1] Lewis's point is fundamental to Christian apologetics: Christianity makes sense in itself, and has the ability to make sense of everything else as well.

Throughout his works—including his works of fiction—Lewis portrays a Christian way of seeing things as habitable, plausible, and persuasive. Once the world has been seen through a Christian set of spectacles, the relative inadequacy of other perspectives becomes clear. One of Lewis's Oxford colleagues, theologian and New Testament scholar Austin Farrer, once noted how Lewis's great strength as an apologist was to be able to bring out how belief in God is both *reasonable* and *natural*.

> [Lewis's] real power was not proof; it was depiction. There lived in his writings a Christian universe that could be both thought and felt, in which he was at home and in which he made his reader feel at home. Moral issues were presented with sharp lucidity and related to the divine will, and once so seen, could never again be seen otherwise.[2]

The intellectual capaciousness of the Christian faith is one of its greatest strengths, and it has considerable apologetic potential—as we shall see in this chapter. In claiming that Christianity makes more sense of reality than anything else, I am not suggesting other viewpoints are irrational. Most forms of atheism, for example, have their own distinct rationality, which some atheists—such as Richard Dawkins and Christopher Hitchens—prematurely and unwisely assume to be the only forms of rationality. Christianity, most apologists suggest, is able to make more sense of things than its alternatives.

A similar point was made by English novelist Evelyn Waugh (1903–66), best known for *Brideshead Revisited* (1945). After his conversion to Christianity in 1930, Waugh wrote to a friend of how his new faith allowed him to see things clearly for the first time.

> Conversion is like stepping across the chimney piece out of a Looking-Glass world, where everything is an absurd caricature, into the real world God made; and then begins the delicious process of exploring it limitlessly.[3]

Before coming to faith, Waugh saw only a distorted world of smoke and mirrors; after his conversion, he saw things for what they really were. He began the process of exploring this new world with excitement, enthusiasm, and wonder, as his later writings make clear.

So how are we to understand the rationality of faith? The reasonableness of the Christian faith can be demonstrated in two different, though clearly complementary, ways:

1. *By showing there is a good argumentative or evidential base for the core beliefs of Christianity.* Such an approach might include developing intellectual arguments for the existence of God, or historical arguments for the resurrection of Jesus of Nazareth. Here, a direct case is made for the reliability of the fundamental elements of the Christian faith.

2. *By showing that, if the Christian faith is true, it makes more sense of reality than its alternatives.* Christianity fits our observations and experiences more plausibly than its alternatives. There is a clear analogy here with the testing of scientific theories, which are usually judged by their ability to accommodate or explain observations.

These two approaches are not mutually exclusive and can be used together in apologetics.

Let us now identify some lines of approach and reflections that are of central importance to apologetics as it seeks to demonstrate the rational plausibility of the Christian faith to our culture.

We can begin our reflections by thinking about the nature of faith.

Understanding the Nature of Faith

The rise of "New Atheism" in 2006 led to a new interest in the nature of faith. Why believe in God, when this cannot be proved with absolute certainty? One of the most familiar New Atheist sound bites was "faith in God is irrational." For militant atheist Richard Dawkins, faith is about running away from evidence, burying your head in the sand, and refusing to think. Although many media observers initially responded positively to these critiques, closer examination has shown them to be remarkably shallow. This New Atheism turns out to have its own unproven—and *unprovable*—beliefs and dogmas, just like every other view.

Philosophical critics of the Enlightenment—such as Alasdair MacIntyre or John Gray—argue that its quest for a universal foundation and criterion of knowledge faltered, stumbled, and finally collapsed under the weight of a massive accumulation of counter-evidence.[4] The vision of a single universal rationality simply could not be defended or achieved. As human beings, we have no choice but to realize we must live in the absence of any clear, unambiguous, absolute, and purely rational truths. We must indeed articulate and defend criteria by which our beliefs may be justified; yet we must also realize those beliefs may lie beyond proof. They are, to use a phrase popularized by Harvard psychologist William James, best understood as "working hypotheses."[5]

An example will help clarify this point. Ethical statements, such as "rape is wrong," cannot be proved to be true, either by reason or science. Nor can political statements, such as "democracy is better than fascism." But this doesn't stop us believing in—and acting on!—such moral and political beliefs. And this applies not just to personal ethics and political viewpoints. It also applies to important social beliefs such as justice. No nation or society can survive without a concept of justice. Yet it turns out we can't *prove*—on the basis of pure human reason—that any specific notion of justice is right.

Michael Sandel, professor of government at Harvard University, recently emphasized that any notion of justice depends upon a conception of the good life, involving a network of beliefs about human nature, values, and purpose.[6] These beliefs, he rightly points out, simply cannot be proved. It is certainly true that some thinkers of the Enlightenment—that great period in western culture that proclaimed the supreme authority of reason—held that reason could indeed answer such questions definitively. But these views have been subjected to severe criticism in the twentieth century. Hardly anyone thinks that now. Questions about justice cannot be meaningfully answered without depending upon beliefs that ultimately cannot be proved. The Enlightenment dream of basing justice on pure reason has foundered. The idea of "pure reason" is a fiction; concepts of rationality are shaped by their cultural environments.

As Stephen Toulmin rightly points out:

> The exercise of rational judgment is itself an activity carried out in a particular context and essentially dependent on it; the arguments we encounter are set out at a given time and in a given situation, and when we come to assess them they have to be judged against this background.[7]

Many Enlightenment thinkers appear to have been shielded from this disconcerting fact by the limitations of their historical scholarship, which remained firmly wedded to the classical western tradition. But this illusion has now been shattered. At the end of his brilliant analysis of rational approaches to knowledge and ethics, Alasdair MacIntyre concludes that the sheer diversity of "rational" approaches to justice and ethics leads inevitably to the conclusion that "the legacy of the Enlightenment has been the provision of an ideal of rational justification which it has proved impossible to attain."[8] Reason promises much, yet fails to deliver its benefits.

We could go on listing examples along the same lines. All of them point to the same conclusion, noted some years ago by the great Oxford philosopher and intellectual historian Sir Isaiah Berlin

(1909–97). Berlin argued that human convictions can be broken down into three categories:

1. Those that can be established by empirical observation.
2. Those that can be established by logical deduction.
3. Those that cannot be proved in either of these ways.[9]

The first two categories concern what can be known reliably through the natural sciences on the one hand, and what can be proved through logic and mathematics on the other. "Proof" turns out to be limited to a very narrow category of statements, such as:

$2 + 2 = 4$

The whole is greater than the part.

The chemical formula for water is H_2O.

The first two of these statements can be proved rationally, and the final one scientifically. The third category contains the values and ideas that shape human culture and define human existence—in other words, beliefs that give human life reason, direction, and purpose, and which cannot be proved by reason or science.

What sorts of things? In 1948, the United Nations reaffirmed its "faith in fundamental human rights." Important though this belief might be, the statements of the Universal Declaration of Human Rights cannot be proved, logically or scientifically. Nor can the belief that oppression is evil, or that rape is wrong. You just can't prove these things. But people make them their life's work, believing they are, in the first place, *right* and, in the second, *important*. As British literary critic Terry Eagleton points out in a powerful critique of Richard Dawkins's book *The God Delusion*, "We hold many beliefs that have no unimpeachably rational justification, but are nonetheless reasonable to entertain."[10] Belief in God is one of these.

Philosopher Alvin Plantinga made this point years ago, with reference to the perennial problem of "other minds."[11] You can't absolutely prove that other people have minds. But nobody's unduly bothered about this. It's a safe assumption, and chimes in with the way things seem to be. Plantinga then argues for a parallel between proving the

existence of "other minds" and proving the existence of God. Neither
can be proved, he argues, and good arguments can be raised against
both—but to their defenders, both seem entirely reasonable.

Richard Rorty (1931–2007), probably the greatest American philosopher of the twentieth century, made a similar point in his presi-
dential address to the American Philosophical Society some years
ago, when he pointed out that

> if anyone really believed that the worth of a theory depends on its
> philosophical grounding, then indeed they would be dubious about
> physics, or democracy, until relativism in respect to philosophical
> theories had been overcome. Fortunately, almost nobody believes
> anything of the sort.[12]

His point? That we can commit ourselves to the great worldviews
of our time without absolute proof.

Everyone reasonably believes certain things to be true, while realizing that these beliefs cannot be proved in the strict sense of that
term. Critics of religious beliefs often suggest that "faith" is some
kind of mental illness, limited to religious people. This is simply
wrong. Faith is just part of being human. As the philosopher Julia
Kristeva recently put it: "Whether I belong to a religion, whether I be
agnostic or atheist, when I say 'I believe,' I mean 'I hold as true.' "[13]
Beliefs about God, justice, and human rights all suffer from this al-
leged problem—just to mention three things to which many others
could easily be added.

Atheist writers often fail to take account of the limits under which
human reason has to operate, holding that their own convictions are
rigorous, reliable, and responsible. They don't believe *anything*, they
tell us—they just limit themselves to what is right. Atheist apologist Christopher Hitchens declares boldly that New Atheists such as
himself do not entertain beliefs. "Our belief is not a belief."[14] This is
simply wrong, and I fear Hitchens is deluding himself. His critique
of religion is clearly dependent on certain core beliefs that cannot be
proved. In Hitchens's case, his aggressive criticism of religion rests
on certain moral values (as in "religion is evil" or "God is not good")
that cannot be proved, and that ultimately represent fiduciary com-
mitments. Since Hitchens's critique of religion is primarily moral, he

is obliged to assume certain moral values he is unable to prove. All moral values ultimately rest on beliefs. In the end, Hitchens's critique of Christianity depends upon and expresses his own beliefs—things he believes to be true and assumes some others will believe to be true, but can't actually prove to be true either by logic or science.

Now there is much more to the Christian idea of faith than believing certain things are true. For Christians, faith is not merely *cognitive* ("I believe this is true"), but also *relational* and *existential* ("I trust this person"). It is not just believing that God exists, but discovering that this God is wise, loving, and good—and choosing to commit ourselves to this God as a result. As C. S. Lewis once remarked, you are not faced "with an argument which demands your assent, but with a Person who demands your confidence."[15]

Faith is thus about trust in someone, not just a belief that he or she exists. This point was made by Danish writer Søren Kierkegaard (1813–55), who emphasized that true faith in God was a "qualitative leap" from one way of existing to another. Christian faith is not the mere addition of one extra item to our inventory of the contents of the world—that is, God. It is about realizing and embracing the new "mode of existence" this trust makes possible. Austrian philosopher Ludwig Wittgenstein is widely regarded as one of the twentieth century's great geniuses. He had severe doubts about the point of "proving" God's existence. He had, he declared, never met anyone who came to believe in God as a result of an argument!

This important point was anticipated in the writings of the great American Puritan theologian Jonathan Edwards (1703–58). For Edwards, rational argument has a valuable and important place in Christian apologetics. Yet this could lead simply to a belief that God existed, without any transformative impact. As Edwards notes, some people "yield a kind of assent of their judgments to the truth of the Christian religion from the rational proofs or arguments that are offered to evince it."[16] But this does not necessarily lead to conversion or a "true faith."

Edwards's point is that someone might believe there *is* a God—but not believe *in* this God. It is a point familiar from the New Testament. "You believe that God is one; you do well. Even the demons believe—and shudder" (James 2:19). There is a world of difference between rational acceptance and personal transformation. What converts people is not an argument, Edwards declares, but an "apprehension"—that is, an informed appreciation—of God's glory, or a direct encounter with or experience of God.

> [Arguments] may be greatly serviceable to awaken unbelievers, and bring them to serious consideration, and to confirm the faith of true saints; yea, they may be in some respect subservient to the begetting of a saving faith in men. Though what was said before remains true, that there is no spiritual conviction of the judgment, but what arises from an apprehension of the spiritual beauty and glory of divine things.[17]

Yet conversion is ultimately the task of evangelism. Apologetics is about preparing the way for such a conversion by showing that it makes sense to believe in God. It's about clearing away rubble and debris in the path of evangelism. We may not be able to prove—in the absolutely rigorous sense of the word—that there is a God. But we can certainly show that it is entirely reasonable to believe such a God exists, in that it makes more sense of life, history, and our experience than anything else—and then we can invite someone to respond to this loving God and trust this God's promises.

Why Does the Reasonableness of Christianity Matter?

Why is this point so important? Why should we need to show that Christian belief is reasonable? Why not just assert it? One of the apologetic points we need to emphasize here is that it is difficult to defend ideas that seem countercultural—going against the grain of dominant cultural ways of thinking. Austin Farrer once suggested that C. S. Lewis's remarkable success as an apologist was partly due to his ability to offer "a positive exhibition of the force of Christian ideas, morally, imaginatively, and rationally."[18] For Farrer, Lewis's approach to apologetics showed how Christianity made sense of the deepest intuitions of the human mind, heart, and imagination.

Yet Farrer was particularly concerned to emphasize the importance of showing the reasonableness of faith. By this, Farrer did not mean that reason created faith, or that people came to believe in God on account of rational arguments. Rather, he wanted to emphasize how it is very difficult to defend the Christian faith publicly if it is seen to be irrational. Lewis's great achievement, according to Farrer, was to demonstrate the reasonableness of faith in a way that facilitated its cultural acceptance.

> Though argument does not create conviction, the lack of it destroys belief. What seems to be proved may not be embraced; but what no one shows the ability to defend is quickly abandoned. Rational argument does not create belief, but it maintains a climate in which belief may flourish.[19]

To demonstrate the reasonableness of faith does not mean proving every article of faith. Rather, it means being able to demonstrate that there are good grounds for believing these articles are trustworthy and reliable—for example, by showing that the Christian faith makes sense of what we observe and experience. The Christian faith can thus be compared to a lens that brings things into focus, or a light that allows us to see farther and more clearly than we can manage on our own.

This point was emphasized by French philosopher and social activist Simone Weil, a Jewish thinker who discovered Christianity as an adult. As she reflected on the implications of her newfound faith, she came to the conclusion that faith in God illuminates reality in a far better way than its secular alternatives. The ability of a way of thinking to bring things into focus, or illuminate what is otherwise dark and obscure, is an indication of its reliability.

> If I light an electric torch at night out of doors I don't judge its power by looking at the bulb, but by seeing how many objects it lights up. The brightness of a source of light is appreciated by the illumination it projects upon non-luminous objects. The value of a religious or, more generally, a spiritual way of life is appreciated by the amount of illumination thrown upon the things of this world.[20]

The ability of a theory to illuminate reality and bring it into sharp focus is itself an important measure of its reliability. We see here a core theme of Christian apologetics: there are good reasons for believing Christianity is true, and one of them is the extent to which it makes sense of what we see around and within us. As Oxford philosopher Brian Leftow commented on his own conversion to Christianity, it seemed to allow things to be seen as they really were: "If you see things as they are from the place where you're standing, you're standing in the right place."[21]

So what about the sciences? Physicist-turned-theologian John Polkinghorne (b. 1930) makes a point of obvious relevance to our concerns in this chapter:

> No form of human truth-seeking enquiry can attain absolute certainty about its conclusions. The realistic aspiration is that of attaining the best explanation of complex phenomena, a goal to be achieved by searching for an understanding sufficiently comprehensive and well-motivated as to afford the basis for rational commitment. Neither science nor religion can entertain the hope of establishing logically coercive proof of the kind that only a fool could deny.[22]

Both science and Christian belief are committed to finding the best evidence-based explanation of what is actually observed and encountered in the world. For the Christian, apologetics is partly about affirming the conceptual resonance between the Christian theoretical framework and the deeper structures of the world, as uncovered by the natural sciences.

So does belief in God make sense? Or is it simply a delusion, a sad example of wish fulfillment on the part of lonely and longing human beings? As Lewis himself once commented, reflecting on his early beliefs as an atheist: "Nearly all that I loved I believed to be imaginary; nearly all that I believed to be real I thought grim and meaningless."[23] This issue has gained importance recently because of present debates in our culture. Although New Atheism, which burst onto the scene in 2006, has now lost much of its novelty value, the questions it raises continue to be discussed. Is belief in God a rational response to reality, or an outmoded delusion spread throughout the population by viruses of the mind, based on flimsy and naïve reasoning, and imposed by authoritarian institutions and individuals?

There is, of course, a more radical viewpoint: *all* human attempts—whether theist or atheist—to construct meaning or establish values are equally delusional. This decidedly bleak view of reality is found at many points in the writings of Richard Dawkins—as in his famous declaration that "the universe we observe has precisely the properties we should expect if there is, at bottom, no design, no purpose, no evil and no good, nothing but blind pitiless indifference."[24] We impose meaning and value on a meaningless universe. Meaning is invented, not discerned. This thought, as consistent as it is austere, is found by many to be unbearable.

In this chapter, we are considering the capacity of the Christian faith to make sense of things. In choosing to focus on the question of its rationality, I am not reducing Christianity to a rational explanation of things, nor implying that this is the chief of its theological virtues. I am simply making the point that our present cultural context has been shaped by the rise of aggressive assertions of the fundamental *irrationality* of faith, and it is therefore necessary to respond to these assertions in a measured and informed way.

The twentieth century saw a new intellectual energy injected into philosophical discussions of the rational and empirical evidence for God, partly catalyzed by new scientific understandings of the origins of the universe. Philosophers of religion such as Alvin Plantinga and Richard Swinburne reaffirmed the rationality of faith and reinvigorated traditional debates about reasons for belief in God. There is a growing consensus that belief in God is perfectly rational—unless, of course, you define "rationality" in terms that deliberately exclude such a belief.[25]

Yet it has become increasingly clear that reason can actually imprison humanity within a rigid and dogmatic worldview that limits reality to what can be proved rationally. As Isaiah Berlin pointed out, it is significant that the dominant mood in western culture from the late nineteenth century onward has been "the rejection of reason and order as being prison houses of the spirit."[26] To limit oneself to what reason and science can prove is merely to skim the surface of reality and fail to discover the hidden depths beneath.

For Christian writers, religious faith is not a rebellion against reason, but a revolt against the imprisonment of humanity within the cold walls of a rationalist dogmatism. Logic and facts can only "take us so far; then we have to go the rest of the way toward belief."[27] Human logic may be rationally adequate, but it is also existentially deficient. Faith declares that there is more than this—not contradicting, but transcending reason. Faith elicits and invites rational consent, but does not compel it. Faith reaches out to where reason points and does not limit itself to where reason stops.

The Philosophy of Science as a Resource for Apologetics

In narrating the story of his conversion in *Surprised by Joy*, C. S. Lewis makes it clear he did not come to believe in God as the result of a deductive argument, but rather by reflection on his experience. This thought leads us to think about how the methods of the natural sciences might be of apologetic value.

Science proceeds by inference, rather than by the deduction of mathematical proof. A series of observations is accumulated, forcing the deeper question: What must be true if we are to explain what is observed? What "big picture" of reality offers the best fit to what is actually observed in our experience? American scientist and philosopher Charles S. Peirce used the term "abduction" to refer to the way in which scientists generate theories that might offer the best explanation of things. The method is now more often referred to as "inference to the best explanation." It is now widely agreed to be the philosophy of investigation of the world characteristic of the natural sciences. So how does it work?

Peirce sets out the process of thinking that leads to the development of new scientific theories or ways of thinking about reality as follows:

1. The surprising fact, C, is observed;
2. But if A were true, C would be a matter of course.
3. Hence, there is reason to suspect that A is true.[28]

Abduction is the process by which we observe certain things and work out what intellectual framework might make sense of them. The great fictional detective Sherlock Holmes used this same method, although he mistakenly called it "deduction." Sometimes, Peirce suggests, abduction "comes to us like a flash, as an 'act of insight.' "[29] Sometimes, it comes about through slow, methodical reflection, as we try to generate every possibility that might make sense of what we observe.

Peirce gives close thought to how scientists develop their ideas, and identifies this process as underlying the scientific method. Science begins by assembling a series of observations, then goes on to ask what framework of interpretation makes most sense of what is observed. It might be a theory passed down from an earlier age. Or it might be a completely new way of thinking. The question that needs to be answered is: How good is the fit between theory and observation? The phrase "empirical fit" is often used to refer to this correspondence between what is seen in the world and what can be accommodated by a theory.

For example, consider the movements of the planets against the starry heavens. These have been observed for thousands of years. But what was the best way of making sense of them? In the Middle Ages, it was thought that the best explanation for these observations was the "Ptolemaic" model, which held that the earth stands at the center of all things, so the sun, moon, and planets all revolve around the earth. By the end of the Middle Ages, it was clear that the observations didn't fit the theory well enough. The Ptolemaic model was groaning and creaking, unable to accommodate increasingly accurate and detailed observational evidence about the movements of the planets. It became clear that a new approach was needed.

In the sixteenth century, Nicolas Copernicus and Johannes Kepler proposed that all the planets, including the earth, rotated around the sun. This "heliocentric" model proved much more successful at making sense of the movements of the planets against the night sky. The close empirical fit between theory and observation strongly suggested that this theory was right. It is still the standard model adopted by astronomers.

But it's not just science that works this way. Peirce himself was clear that trial lawyers also depend on abduction for their professional successes. They must develop a theoretical lens that illuminates the evidence and brings it into sharp focus. The criminal justice system involves reaching agreement on the best explanation of the evidence laid before the courts. What is the "big picture" that makes best sense of the evidence? In the end, the theory that will persuade a jury is going to be the one that weaves as many of the clues as possible together into a coherent narrative.

We see here the quest for the big picture that makes sense of individual snapshots, the grand narrative that makes sense of individual stories, and the grand theory that connects the clues together into a satisfying and coherent whole. For what applies to scientific and legal theories also applies to our attempts to make sense of life as a whole—above all, to the question of God and human meaning. How can these approaches help with the apologetic task?

There are three main types of scientific explanation, each of which has considerable value in relation to apologetics: causal explanation, inference to the best explanation, and unificatory explanation. In what follows, we shall consider the apologetic potential of each of these.

1. Explanation as the identification of causes.

The first type of explanation is causal. Perhaps the most familiar approach to scientific explanation, this argues that A explains B if it can be shown that A causes B.[30] So does this mean Christians believe God pokes around in nature, nudging apples so they fall from trees and then pulling them to the ground? No. God delegates causal efficacy to the created order. Thomas Aquinas develops the notion of "secondary causality" as an extension of, not an alternative to, the primary causality of God himself. Events within the created order can exist in complex causal relationships, without in any way refuting their ultimate dependency upon God as final cause.[31]

The critical point to appreciate is that the created order thus demonstrates causal relationships that can be investigated by the natural sciences. Those causal relationships can be investigated and correlated—for example, in the form of the "laws of nature"—without in any way implying, and still less necessitating, an atheistic worldview. To put this as simply as possible: God creates a world with its own ordering and processes.

But what of the origins of the universe? In the late nineteenth century, scientists tended to think of the universe as always having existed. Yet in the twentieth century, it became increasingly clear that the universe came into being in a massive explosion usually known as "the big bang."[32] Since the realization that the universe had a beginning, the philosophy of science has struggled to find an explanation of how something could come into existence from nothing. How can nothing be said to cause something? The widespread acceptance that the universe had a chronological origin significantly shifted the ground in favor of belief in a "first cause" and an intelligent designer. What caused the universe to appear? Perhaps the cosmos created itself. Perhaps it just happened. Or perhaps it was brought into creation by an agent—such as God. This *proves* nothing, of course, in the logically rigorous sense of the term. But it does give a new credibility to one of the most familiar traditional arguments for the existence of God, which can be set out like this:

1. Whatever begins to exist has a cause.
2. The universe began to exist.
3. Therefore the universe has a cause.

2. The quest for the best explanation.

Since about 1970, it has been widely accepted that the fundamental philosophy of the natural sciences is the approach widely known as "inference to the best explanation."[33] The basic approach here is to ask this question: Which theory makes the most sense of what we actually observe in nature? There is an important debate in the philosophical literature over how you work out which is the best explanation: is it the simplest, the most elegant, or the most fertile? What "big picture" of things best corresponds to the evidence? Charles Darwin's development of his theory of "natural selection" is now seen as a textbook case of this approach.

Two points stand out as being of supreme importance here. First, this approach recognizes that you can't *prove* which is the best explanation. This is a matter of fiduciary judgment—of *discernment*—within the scientific community. We see this in the present scientific debate over the "multiverse," where two radically different explanations are advanced for the same observations. Each has gathered support within the scientific community. But nobody really knows which is right. You have to decide which you believe to be right, on the basis of the evidence available—and realize the evidence isn't conclusive enough to prove either option. (It's inconvenient, but at least it means you treat your opponents with courtesy, instead of declaring they are deluded.)

Second, "inference to the best explanation" recognizes that there are potentially lots of ways of explaining things, and tries to agree to a framework by which competing claims can be resolved. Very rarely is it possible to prove a theory is right. But this isn't always necessary. It's just necessary to show that a theory is better than its rivals. To put this another way, many scientific theories can be said to be warranted or justified (in other words, have a good evidential basis), without thereby being proved.

God fits into this way of thinking with remarkable ease. Oxford philosopher of religion Richard Swinburne, for example, argues that belief in God provides the best explanation of a wide range of things we observe in the world.[34] In a similar vein, physicist John Polkinghorne notes that belief in God offers an explanation of "meta-theoretical" questions—beliefs on which science is obliged to depend but cannot itself demonstrate to be true.

3. Explanation as the unification of our view of reality.

Since about 1990, there has been growing interest within the philosophy of science in the notion of "explanatory unification." This approach to scientific explanation has its origins in the 1970s, and tries to establish a common framework for what were once thought to be unrelated events.[35] Since then, the method has been developed extensively and used to explain some core features of the development of the modern scientific method.[36] Its basic theme is simple: we need to find a framework big enough to accommodate as much as possible.

This way of understanding scientific explanation is based on the observation that aspects of reality once believed to require different kinds of explanation can actually be accommodated within the same explanatory framework. James Clerk Maxwell's famous demonstration of the unity of electricity and magnetism is an obvious example of this approach. Electricity and magnetism, once thought to be totally distinct, could be seen as two sides of the same coin. To explain something is to locate it within a wider context, allowing its interconnectedness to other aspects of reality to be understood. The question concerns which network of ideas establishes the maximum degree of interconnection between different scientific domains and theories.

It is not difficult to see how this resonates strongly with a central theme of the Christian faith. For Augustine of Hippo, God was like an intellectual sun illuminating the landscape of reality, allowing us to see its deep structures and to figure out our own place within them. A similar theme is found in the writings of C. S. Lewis.

Making Sense of Things: A Case Study

To explore this further, we shall consider how effective the Christian way of seeing things is at making sense of what we observe. How good is the fit between theory and observation?

So how can we make sense of the shape of history and the distinctive features of human culture? A number of controlling narratives have been proposed to make sense of these. One of them, favored by New Atheism, is that of the progressive improvement of the human condition through the erosion of religious superstition, and the emancipation of humanity from all taboos and arbitrary limits. It has recently become much more difficult to sustain this metanarrative in the West, as the manifest failings of western liberalism have become increasingly clear. Indeed, it is significant that this metanarrative is one of the chief targets of Eagleton's recent withering critique of New Atheism.

Eagleton describes the "dream of untrammeled human progress" as a "bright-eyed superstition," a fairy tale lacking any rigorous evidential base. "If ever there was a pious myth and a piece of credulous superstition, it is the liberal-rationalist belief that, a few hiccups apart, we are all steadily en route to a finer world."[37] It is interesting that Christopher Hitchens ends his polemic against religion with a plea for a return to the Enlightenment, especially the form it took in the eighteenth century. The myth of a lost golden age, it seems, persists in this most unlikely of quarters. Yet we are surely called to question fictions about both human individuals and society, even if these fictions are deeply embedded within the secular western mindset.

The New Atheist grand story (or metanarrative) is that of the former enslavement of humanity to primitive superstitions. Through the intelligent application of reason and science in the last few centuries, humanity was able to break free from this age-old oppression and enter a bright new world of liberty and enlightenment—a bright new world that is now threatened by the reemergence of what are darkly referred to as "superstition" and "irrationalism." Religion has made an expected and unwelcome comeback. Something needs to be done to restore the situation before it is too late!

Like all the best stories, this narrative has the virtue of simplicity.
Yet it quickly loses value when it proves incapable of accommodat-
ing history as a whole, rather than a few carefully selected snippets.
Religion was meant to have died out in the West years ago. During
the 1960s, European sociologists predicted the imminent advent of
a secularist world order with much the same confidence as an earlier
generation of Soviet political theorists proclaimed the historical
inevitability of Marxism-Leninism. "The most illustrious figures
in sociology, anthropology and psychology" unanimously declared
that "their children—or surely their grandchildren—would live to see
the dawn of a new era in which, to paraphrase Freud, the infantile
illusions of religion would be outgrown."[38]

Except religion hasn't disappeared. Many now argue that it is
more influential than ever, despite the social controls being used
to minimize its social impact within much of western Europe. The
Soviet Union has fallen apart, its enforced secularism now replaced
by a religiously active and zealous group of nations. And that's
what's frightening the New Atheists. Their metanarrative is facing
a challenge. It doesn't work.

The Enlightenment metanarrative fails to explain anything important. As Richard Shweder recently pointed out, it has "a predictive
capacity of approximately zero."[39] Religion might turn out to be a
delusion, Shweder dryly remarked—but it seems to be a delusion with
a future. "The popularity of the current counterattack on religion
cloaks a renewed and intense anxiety within secular society that it
is not the story of religion but rather the story of the Enlightenment
that may be more illusory than real."[40]

The Enlightenment story of meaning, on which New Atheism is
so dependent, now looks about as realistic as the earlier Marxist assertion of the historic inevitability of socialism. The resurgence of
religion in many parts of the world where it was repressed by atheistic
governments is an obvious indication of the vulnerability and fragility
of this story of meaning. In any case, the idea of "historical inevitability" is really a *sociological* judgment, which has little to do with what
is intellectually or morally right or wrong.[41] Whether a sociological
development is "inevitable" or not has little bearing on whether it is
right. A cultural or historical development may be inevitable only as
a *passing historical phase*, rather than as a permanent development.

New Atheism often accuses those who believe in God of holding on to "unevidenced beliefs," in contrast to the rigorously proven factual statements of "enlightened" atheists. Yet what of its own belief in human progress? Eagleton dismisses this myth as a demonstrably false pastiche, a luminous example of "blind faith."[42] What rational soul would sign up to such a secular myth, which is obliged to treat such human created catastrophes as Hiroshima, Auschwitz, and apartheid as "a few local hiccups" that in no way discredit or disrupt the steady upward progress of history? The difference between Christianity and New Atheism seems to lie in their choice of so-called unevidenced beliefs and controlling myths. Neither can be proved; this, however, does not prevent us from making an adjudication about which appears to be the more reliable and compelling.

So what of a Christian reading of culture and history? Two controlling themes here are the ideas of humanity as, first, created in the "image of God" and, second, sinful. While theologians and religious communities differ in the relative emphasis placed upon these two elements of a Christian understanding of human nature, they are nevertheless the twin poles of any Christian attempt to make sense of the enigmas and puzzles of how we behave, as individuals and in society.

We find ourselves excited and inspired by the vision of God, which draws us upward; we find ourselves pulled down by the frailty and fallenness of human nature. It is a familiar dilemma, famously articulated by Paul: "I do not do the good I want, but the evil I do not want is what I do" (Rom. 7:19). From a Christian perspective, it is clear we must recognize at one and the same time a greater destiny or capacity in humanity than most political systems or philosophies allow, and a correspondingly great capacity to fail to achieve such aspirations.

This way of thinking allows us to frame the complex picture we see of human culture and history, characterized by aspirations to greatness and goodness on the one hand, and oppression and violence on the other. Many have commented on the profound ambiguity of history and the havoc it wreaks for naïve theories of the goodness of humanity. Terry Eagleton is only one of a series of recent commentators to point out the darker side of contemporary human culture and history.

As a species, humanity may indeed have the capacity for good; this seems matched, however, by a capacity for evil. A recognition of this profound ambiguity is essential if we are to avoid political and social utopianism based on naïve, ideologically driven, nonempirical value judgments about human nature. As J. R. R. Tolkien wrote so presciently in 1931, on the eve of the rise of Nazism, a naïve view of humanity leads to political utopianism, in which "progress" potentially leads to catastrophe:

> I will not walk with your progressive ages,
> Erect and sapient. Before them gapes
> the dark abyss to which their progress tends.[43]

Moving On

In this chapter, we have reflected on the apologetic importance of demonstrating the "reasonableness" of faith. Nobody wants to embrace a faith that is utterly mad! Some Christians suggest that, since Paul speaks of the gospel as a form of "foolishness" that confounds worldly knowledge and wisdom (e.g., 1 Cor. 1:18), there is no point in using rational means to defend the gospel. Yet this clearly represents a misreading of Paul's concerns about the situation in Corinth on the one hand, and his understanding of the role of the "mind" in the Christian life on the other.

Paul's concerns at Corinth were complex.[44] The church was in danger of being influenced by early forms of Gnosticism, which held that individuals were saved by a secret, arcane knowledge. Others at Corinth prized intellectual sophistication and were not prepared to tolerate anything that seemed to lack this or any other mark of cultural erudition. Paul rightly rejects any such notions, insisting the Christian gospel must be taken on its own terms, even if it counters prevailing cultural notions of acceptability at Corinth. Yet this is about challenging secular notions of wisdom, not abandoning human notions of rationality!

Paul insists that Christians "have the mind of Christ" (1 Cor. 2:16), which he distinguishes from alternative approaches to wisdom already present at Corinth. A "Christian mind" is a distinctive mindset, a way of thinking shaped and nourished by the Christian faith. It is not about a quest for exotic or arcane knowledge, nor the exaltation of academic arrogance, nor a lapse into the discredited rationalism of eighteenth-century Enlightenment. It is about allowing the light of Christ to shine upon our intellects, so that the transforming power of God's grace might renew our minds as well as our souls. It is the outcome encouraged and intended by God as we seek to serve him in the world.

So how does the gospel make sense of things? How are we to understand and apply its deep appeal to our reason, feelings, imagination, and longing for meaning? In the following chapter, we shall consider eight major lines of apologetic engagement, each of which has its own role to play in helping the gospel gain a foothold in contemporary culture.

For Further Reading

Evans, C. Stephen. *Natural Signs and Knowledge of God: A New Look at Theistic Arguments*. New York: Oxford University Press, 2010.

McGrath, Alister E. *Surprised by Meaning: Science, Faith, and How We Make Sense of Things*. Louisville, Westminster John Knox, 2011.

Morris, Thomas V., ed. *God and the Philosophers: The Reconciliation of Faith and Reason*. Oxford: Oxford University Press, 1994.

Swinburne, Richard. *The Existence of God*, 2nd ed. Oxford: Clarendon Press, 2004.

Wright, N. T. *Simply Christian: Why Christianity Makes Sense*. San Francisco: HarperSanFrancisco, 2006.

6

Pointers to Faith

APPROACHES TO APOLOGETIC ENGAGEMENT

merican poet Edna St. Vincent Millay (1892–1950) spoke of "a meteoric shower of facts" raining from the sky. These facts are like threads that need to be woven into a tapestry, clues that need to be assembled to disclose the big picture. As Millay pointed out, we are overwhelmed with information, but cannot make sense of the "shower of facts" with which we are bombarded. There seems to be "no loom to weave it into fabric." We need a way of making sense of this shower of information. Christianity gives us a way of bringing order and intelligibility to our many and complex observations of the natural world, human history, and personal experience. It allows us to integrate them, and see them as interconnected aspects of a greater whole.

We want to see the big picture that makes sense of all we observe. More importantly, we want to know where we fit into this great scheme of things. No wonder British philosopher and writer Iris Murdoch (1919–99) spoke of "the calming, whole-making tendencies of human thought," by which she means the ability of a big picture or "grand narrative" to integrate our vision of reality. The Christian faith is about grasping the big picture, enabling us to see a larger and nobler vision of reality than human reason can disclose.

Clues, Pointers, and Proofs

In the previous chapter, we argued that the Christian faith was fundamentally reasonable. It cannot be proved by reason; but then, neither can anything that really matters. Older generations, needlessly submitting to a rather aggressive rationalism, argued that we should believe only what could be proved *absolutely*. That viewpoint is now held by very few people. For most, such vigorous rationalism simply confines us to a very narrow category of beliefs, which may be logically clear but are existentially deficient. They just can't provide a basis for a meaningful life. Reason, as the great Italian poet Dante noted back in the fourteenth century, has short wings.

But this doesn't mean beliefs that cannot be proved absolutely are unreasonable. Far from it. When it comes to theories of life or "worldviews," the evidence available to us just isn't good enough to prove that any of them—including atheism—are right. In the end, we have to make these decisions as a matter of faith. Otherwise we must declare every worldview to lie beyond resolution. We believe our worldview is the best way to make sense of things, but we realize the matter ultimately lies beyond proof here in this world.

For the Christian, this situation has to be seen against the backdrop of belief in heaven. "We live by faith, not by sight" (2 Cor. 5:7 NIV). For now, we walk through a shadow land, but one day the sun will rise, and we will see things as they really are. "For salvation is nearer to us now than when we became believers; the night is far gone, the day is near" (Rom. 13:11–12). These phrases from Paul invite us to think of the Christian life as walking in the dark. The dawn is nearer than when we first began this walk, but it has yet to happen. In the meantime we have to cross an unknown landscape, hoping we will arrive safely at our destination. We cannot fully see the road ahead of us; nevertheless, we trust in the Lord to guide us home. As Paul famously puts it, "For now we see in a mirror, dimly, but then we will see face to face. Now I know only in part; then I will know fully, even as I have been fully known" (1 Cor. 13:12).

Yet we are not being asked to take things on blind trust. The world is studded with clues about human nature and identity. Reality is emblazoned with signs pointing to the greater reality of God. We need to connect the dots and see the overall picture. We need to weave the threads together and see what pattern they disclose. These patterns are there to be used by the apologist to help others begin to realize how Christianity has the power to make sense of what we think, see, and experience—and to encourage them to discover Christianity's deeper power to transform human life.

It is not only the external world that might point to God. What of our inner experience? Christian apologetics has the capacity to connect, powerfully and credibly, with the dynamics of inner human subjectivity—in other words, with the feelings and emotions that lie at the heart of so many of our concerns, which so excited the Romantic poets and other writers such as Blaise Pascal and C. S. Lewis. What has the Christian faith to say about these? How can we view our inner experience through its theoretical lens? The Christian tradition has explored this question from its origins. In his *Confessions*, Augustine of Hippo relates how his reading of "the Platonists" led him to explore his own inwardness, and there he encountered "an immutable light, higher than my mind."[1]

In this chapter, we shall consider some of these pointers or signs and explore how they can be used in apologetics. C. S. Lewis spoke of right and wrong as "clues to the meaning of the universe." A clue is something that suggests, but does not prove. Clues have a cumulative significance, pointing to a deeper pattern of meaning that gives each of them their true meaning. One clue on its own might be nothing more than suggestive, a straw in the wind. Yet a cluster of clues begins to disclose a comprehensive pattern. Each clue builds on the others, giving them a collective force that transcends their individual importance.

So how can we best make sense of such clues? What can they prove? In a criminal trial, the jury is asked to decide which explanation of the clues makes the most sense of them—whether that of the prosecution or the defense. They are not expected to accept that guilt or innocence has been proved, merely that they believe they can reach a conclusion "beyond reasonable doubt." Apologetics works in much the same way. No one is going to be able to prove the existence of God, as one might prove that "the whole is greater than the part." Yet one can consider all the clues that point in this direction and take pleasure in their cumulative force. God's existence may not be *proved*, in the hard rationalist sense of the word. Yet it can be affirmed with complete sincerity that belief in God is eminently reasonable and makes more sense of what we see in the world, discern in history, and experience in our lives than its alternatives.

So what sort of clues are we talking about? And how can the apologist help people see them, reflect on their importance, and discern the deeper pattern behind them? In this chapter we shall consider eight clues to the mystery of life. Each can be studied on its own and can form the basis of an apologetic talk or argument. We'll begin by considering one of the most intriguing questions in the natural sciences: Where did the universe come from?

Clue 1: Creation—The Origins of the Universe

A central theme of the Christian faith is that God created all things from nothing. Everything owes its origins and ultimate identity to the creative action of God. The universe has not existed from all eternity, but came into being in an instant. Christian writers have taken a variety of positions on how this fundamental belief is to be understood. Augustine of Hippo, for example, argues that God created the universe instantaneously but endowed it with a capacity for subsequent development. Others argue that God created the world in its present form. Yet the common thread uniting all Christian writers on this theme is that God brought the universe into existence.

Although New Atheist propagandists regularly declare that scientific advance and progress has eroded the case for belief in God in the last century, the facts are otherwise. The relation of science and faith changed decisively in the later twentieth century. The first decades of the twentieth century were dominated by a scientific belief in the eternity of the universe. It had always existed. Religious language about "creation" was seen as mythological nonsense, incompatible with cutting-edge scientific knowledge.

This belief played an important role in the great 1948 London debate between two leading philosophers—atheist Bertrand Russell (1872–1970) and Christian Frederick C. Coplestone (1907–90). Russell believed that this scientific consensus was more than sufficient to put an end to the whole God debate once and for all. The universe is just there, and there's no good reason to think about what brought it into being. At least on this point, Russell won the debate.

But everything has changed since 1948. During the 1960s, it became increasingly clear that the universe had an origin—the so-called big bang. This idea was met with fierce resistance by some atheist scientists of the day, such as the great atheist astrophysicist Fred Hoyle, who was worried that this idea sounded uncomfortably religious. He wasn't alone in worrying about this. At a meeting in Leningrad in December 1948, Soviet astronomers affirmed the need to fight against the "reactionary-idealistic" theory of the universe having an origin. Support for this theory would, the Soviets claimed, help the cause of "clericalism."[2]

Happily, this prejudice against the idea of the universe having an origin was overwhelmed by the evidence in its favor. But the fact remains: the new understanding of the origins of the universe resonate strongly with the Christian doctrine of creation. The universe had a beginning.

If the Russell-Coplestone debate were to take place again today, its outcome would be very different at this point. In fact, a replay of the Russell-Coplestone debate was staged between two leading philosophers in 1998 to mark its 50th anniversary, featuring Christian William Lane Craig and then-atheist Anthony Flew. Craig, the philosopher whom many now regard as Coplestone's natural successor, developed the following line of argument, which we noted earlier (p. 85):

Major premise: Whatever begins to exist has a cause.
Minor premise: The universe began to exist.
Conclusion: Therefore the universe has a cause.

Unusually, here the minor premise is at least as important as, and possibly even more important than, the major premise. Craig's minor premise, accepted today by virtually every scientist, would have been equally comprehensively rejected in 1948. Flew experienced considerable difficulty at this point, and was unable to deploy with plausibility the strategies used by earlier generations of atheist apologists. Since this debate, Flew moved away from atheism. Although it would not be correct to say that Flew adopted the full richness of the Christian vision of God, there is no doubt that before his death in 2010 he came to accept the existence of a creator God who sustains the universe.

This fundamental shift in the scientific consensus has changed the tone of the debate about God. It reminds us how science changes its mind about things—often very important things. The cosmology of the early twenty-first century is much more sympathetic to Christian belief than that of a century ago. But there is more to it than this. There is now a growing realization that the universe came into being fine-tuned for life. The fundamental constants of nature have values that seem to have been selected in order to allow life to develop. Is this just a cosmic accident? Or is it what would be expected if God had chosen to work in this way?

Clue 2: Fine-Tuning—A Universe Designed for Life?

In recent years, increasing attention has been paid to the phenomenon of "fine-tuning" in nature.[3] The term "fine-tuning" is often used to refer to the scientific realization that the values of certain fundamental cosmological constants and the character of certain initial conditions of the universe appear to have played a decisive role in bringing about the emergence of a particular kind of universe, one within which intelligent life can develop. Many recent scientific studies have emphasized the significance of certain fundamental cosmological constants, the values of which, if varied even slightly, would have significant implications for the emergence of human existence.[4]

Nature's fundamental constants turn out to have been fine-tuned to reassuringly life-friendly values. The existence of carbon-based life on earth depends upon a delicate balance of physical and cosmological forces and parameters. Were any one of these quantities slightly altered, balance would have been destroyed and life would not have come into existence. Sir Martin Rees, Britain's Astronomer Royal and President of the Royal Society, has argued that the emergence of human life in the aftermath of the big bang is governed by a mere six numbers, each of which is so precisely determined that a miniscule variation in any one of them would have made both our universe and human life, as we know them, impossible.[5]

A recent discussion of this question by Robert J. Spitzer is helpful here. Spitzer suggests we imagine all the parameters of the universe—such as the speed of light in a vacuum, the gravitational constant, electromagnetic coupling, and the masses of the elementary particles—are represented by the settings of the dials of some kind of "cosmic control panel."[6] The findings of modern cosmology imply that if the settings of these dials were to be nudged even very slightly, we would not be here to discuss their significance. For example, if gravity or the weak force (two of the four known forces of nature) were to be varied in strength by one part in 10^{40}, the expansion of the universe would either be too explosive for galaxies or the universe would have collapsed. If a certain combination of the constants of gravity, electromagnetism, and the ratio of electron to proton mass were varied by about one part in 10^{39}, no main sequence stars such as our own sun would be able to form. If a precise nuclear resonance of the carbon atom did not align with the resonance of beryllium and a colliding helium nucleus (yet without aligning with a corresponding resonance in oxygen and helium), then there would be almost no carbon, the basis of life as we know it. Most dramatically, leading mathematician Roger Penrose has calculated that the entropy of the universe is such that our universe seems to exist in an absurdly precise state compared to the available range of possible values. So what are the apologetic implications of this remarkable fine-tuning?

The phenomenon of fine-tuning is widely conceded; all debates concern its *interpretation*. Atheist cosmologist Fred Hoyle was one of those to first appreciate the importance of these observations and their obvious theistic implications. It is, he wrote, as if "a super-intellect has monkeyed with physics, as well as with chemistry and biology, and . . . there are no blind forces worth speaking about in nature."[7] Hoyle was an atheist, unsympathetic to the idea that God created the universe. Nevertheless, his comment points to the deep unease contemporary cosmology has created for those not willing to believe in God. Might the evidence be better explained by the idea of divine creation than by happenstance? Hoyle certainly hoped not—but it rather looked that way to him.

One way of trying to avoid the obvious theistic implications of fine-tuning is to postulate a "multiverse." This viewpoint argues that our own universe is only one option among many others. The observable universe is thus to be contextualized within an unseen, infinitely larger, and eternal multiverse. Our own universe may be fine-tuned; but none of the others need be. We're just lucky. Someone had to hit the jackpot. No wonder Richard Dawkins favors this approach!

But there are obvious problems with the multiverse hypothesis, as Spitzer rightly points out.[8] First, the distinction between universe and multiverse is largely semantic. There is still just one true universe in this hypothesis, if the term "universe" means the entire domain of interconnected physical reality. If the hypothetical multiverse is not connected in any way to the particular universe that we actually observe, it is difficult to see how any laws of physics derived in our domain could possibly apply to the multiverse as a whole. This means we cannot use observations of our own world to draw any conclusions about the multiverse at all. But if the multiverse is structurally interconnected, many problems encountered with the big bang theory are simply displaced, reappear in a modified form, or even become more difficult for atheists.

So what is the apologetic significance of this? The observation of fine-tuning is consonant with Christian belief in a creator God. It *proves* nothing; after all, this might just have been an extremely improbable accident. Nevertheless, it resonates strongly with the Christian way of thinking, fitting easily and naturally into the map of reality that emerges from the Christian faith. The capacity of Christianity to map these phenomena is not conclusive proof of anything. It is, however, highly suggestive. It is one among many clues, accumulating to give an overall "big picture" of reality. It is one among many threads that can be woven together to yield a patterned tapestry. Fine-tuning is a clue to the meaning of the universe, insignificant in isolation but richly suggestive when set alongside other such clues.

For the Christian, there is a deep conceptual resonance between the Christian theoretical framework and the way the world is, as uncovered by the natural sciences. We shall consider this further as we reflect on a third clue to the meaning of the universe: the deep structure of the world.

Clue 3: Order—The Structure of the Physical World

Our instinct to discern order within the world is expressed clearly in the wisdom literature of the Old Testament. The natural sciences are also based on the idea of the regularity of the universe. Without an ordered cosmos, the scientific enterprise would be impossible.

My own time as a scientist impressed upon me the privilege of being able to investigate a universe that is both rationally transparent and rationally beautiful, capable of being represented in elegant mathematical forms. One of the most significant parallels between the natural sciences and Christian theology is a fundamental conviction that the world is characterized by regularity and intelligibility. As one modern cosmologist has noted, "The God of the physicists is cosmic order."[9] There is something special about the world—and the nature of the human mind—that allows patterns within nature to be discerned and represented.

One of the most significant parallels between the natural sciences and Christian theology is a basic belief that the world is regular and intelligible. This perception of ordering and intelligibility is of immense significance both at the scientific and religious levels. As physicist Paul Davies points out, "In Renaissance Europe, the justification for what we today call the scientific approach to inquiry was the belief in a rational God whose created order could be discerned from a careful study of nature."[10]

God has created an ordered world, an order capable of being discerned by humanity, who have in turn been created "in the image and likeness of God." Why can human beings discern this ordering? Why are we able to represent it so elegantly using mathematical equations? As theoretical physicist John Polkinghorne pointed out, this is much more significant than is usually appreciated:

> We are so familiar with the fact that we can understand the world that most of the time we take it for granted. It is what makes science possible. Yet it could have been otherwise. The universe might have been a disorderly chaos rather than an orderly cosmos. Or it might have had a rationality which was inaccessible to us. . . . There is a congruence between our minds and the universe, between the rationality experienced within and the rationality observed without.[11]

So why is the universe so intelligible to us? How can we account for its rational transparency? Why is there such a deep-seated congruence between the rationality present in our minds and the rationality we observe in the world? Why is it that the abstract structures of pure mathematics—which are supposed to be a free creation of the human mind—provide such important clues to understanding the world? The great mathematician Eugene Wigner once famously asked: "Why is mathematics so unreasonably effective in understanding the physical world?"[12] His question needs to be answered. But science cannot answer it. In fact, science depends precisely upon this "unreasonable effectiveness" of mathematics. It uses it as a tool—without being able to offer a theoretical account of why it is so reliable in this way.

Polkinghorne's point is that the Christian faith offers a map of reality that allows us to make sense of these observations. Both the "reason within" and the "reason without"—the rationality of the human mind, and that embedded in the deep structure of the universe—have a common origin in a deeper rationality, the "mind of God." The natural sciences regularly raise important questions that transcend the capacity of the scientific method to answer them. Such questions are often of the greatest interest and importance but go beyond the realms in which science itself is competent to speak. Science is obliged to assume the intelligibility of the world—to depend upon it for its methods. The Christian faith is able to offer an answer to this question of the intelligibility of the world that arises from science yet goes beyond the unaided power of science to answer, and offers a "map of meaning" that makes this profoundly comprehensible.

C. S. Lewis also reflected on why human rationality appears to be so congruent with the structures of the natural world.

> No account of the universe can be true unless that account leaves it possible for our thinking to be a real insight. A theory which explained everything else in the whole universe but which made it impossible to believe that our thinking was valid, would be utterly out of court. For that theory would itself have been reached by thinking, and if thinking is not valid, that theory would, of course, be itself demolished.[13]

The human use of reason to investigate the world thus depends on the rationality of the world. Lewis's argument is that both creation in general, and human reason in particular, bear traces or imprints of the creative ordering of God. The same God who brought the world into being also created the human mind, with a God-given analogy and congruence between both these his creations and his own divine nature.

Why is this approach helpful apologetically? There are a number of points that need to be made here. First, this approach emphasizes the capacity of the Christian faith to make sense of things—to chime in with what is observed in the world, or the deeper picture of reality that emerges from the natural sciences. Second, it offers an important point of contact with the natural sciences. Although science and faith are sometimes presented as being in conflict, it is better to think of faith as offering a deeper context to the scientific method. In other words, it offers an explanation of why science works.

This is of particular importance in relation to the idea of the "God of the gaps," an idea that is sometimes found in older works of apologetics. This approach tries to defend the existence of God by an appeal to gaps in scientific explanation. I must confess that I have never been impressed by this approach. Oxford theoretical chemist Charles Coulson (1910–74) was a vigorous critic of this way of thinking, arguing that "either God is in the whole of Nature, with no gaps, or He's not there at all."[14] Christian apologetics ought not to become preoccupied with looking for temporary explanatory gaps in the scientific view of the world. God is the one who gives meaning to the whole universe, who alone is able to explain why there is anything at all and what it means. Apologetics is about showing how the "big picture" possible through Christianity makes sense of the world.

Clue 4: Morality—A Longing for Justice

One of the great themes of classical philosophy is what is sometimes called the "Platonic triad"—truth, beauty, and goodness. These are ideals that most people recognize as significant and important. The apologist is able to use each of these as a gateway to faith. Each ideal, when properly and carefully applied, can become a window through which the truth, beauty, and goodness of God can be discerned.

Classical apologetics tends to focus on questions of truth. There is much wisdom in such an approach. The human mind seems to have a God-given capacity to make sense of things and to realize we are part of something much bigger. We realize our human processes of reasoning can be seen as participations in and reflections of an objective rational order, established by God and reflecting God's nature and character. Humanity is created in God's image and thus reflects—however dimly!—the rationality of God. We are able to grasp the deeper structure of the universe, including the existence of God, because we have been created to do precisely that. Augustine of Hippo is one classic Christian writer to develop this approach, based on the core biblical insight that we bear God's image (Gen. 1:27).

> The image of the creator is to be found in the rational or intellectual soul of humanity. . . . The human soul has been created according to the image of God in order that it may use reason and intellect in order to apprehend and behold God.[15]

As Augustine, Pascal, and Lewis appreciated, recognizing we are made in the image of God provides a powerful theological foundation for Christian apologetics. It means we are able to use the deep human longing for truth, beauty, and goodness to help people orient themselves toward their ultimate origin and goal—the living and loving God.

Our concern in this section is with "the good"—in other words, with the foundations of a sustainable vision of what is good and how we are to live by it. In a recent radio discussion, a British journalist explored the nature of morality with well-known militant atheist Richard Dawkins. Justin Brierley (JB) asked Dawkins (RD) whether his Darwinian perspective on things offered a reliable foundation for ethical values. The following section of the interview was especially interesting from the standpoint of Christian apologetics:

> JB: But when you make a value judgment, don't you immediately step yourself outside of this evolutionary process and say the reason this is good is because it's good, and you don't have any way to stand on that statement?
>
> RD: But my value judgment itself could come from my evolutionary past.
>
> JB: So therefore it's just as random in a sense as any product of evolution.

RD: Well, you could say that. But it doesn't in any case—nothing about it makes it more probable that there is anything supernatural.

JB: Okay, but ultimately, your belief that rape is wrong is as arbitrary as the fact that we've evolved five fingers rather than six.

RD: You could say that, yeah.[16]

The interview probed one of the most important questions that regularly arises in debate: is morality dependent upon a transcendent norm or ground—such as God? In debate, many atheists dismiss this question as ridiculous. How dare anyone suggest that atheists are immoral because they do not believe in God! But that is not the real issue. The big question is whether an objective morality can be sustained without belief in God. For Christians, God alone offers an objective foundation for moral values, which is not subject to the whims of the powerful or the changing moods of public opinion. Leading atheist philosopher Paul Kurtz puts the point well:

> The central question about moral and ethical principles concerns this ontological foundation. If they are neither derived from God nor anchored in some transcendent ground, are they purely ephemeral?[17]

A historical example will make the force of this point clear. In 1933, the Nazis seized power in Germany and promptly set about using the law to impose totalitarian rule. New laws were brought in that enforced Nazi ideology, so the Nazis could claim they used legal means to impose their ideas. The only way of challenging the Nazi approach was to argue that there existed a higher moral authority than the German state. The situation in Germany at this time highlights an issue that cannot be ignored—namely, whether there are transcendent grounds for concepts of morality and justice that are not merely the product of human convention.

The disturbing questions raised by the rise of the Third Reich and its aftermath have not gone away. Indeed, they have been raised again by a "pragmatic" approach to morality, such as that associated with influential philosopher Richard Rorty (1931–2007). On this reading of things, humanity creates its own values and ideas, and is not accountable to any external objectivity (natural law) or internal subjectivity (conscience) for the outcome of this creative process.

"We figure out what practices to adopt first, and then expect our philosophers to adjust the definition of 'human' or 'rational' to suit."[18] Rorty argues that a consequence of this communitarian or pragmatic approach to truth must be the recognition that

> there is nothing deep down inside us except what we have put there ourselves, no criterion that we have not created in the course of creating a practice, no standard of rationality that is not an appeal to such a criterion, no rigorous argumentation that is not obedience to our own conventions.[19]

Truth and morality thus have to be recognized to reflect social conventions, which are created by human communities. Yet if Rorty is right, what ultimate justification could be given for opposing Nazism? Rorty finds himself unable to offer a persuasive justification for the moral or political rejection of totalitarianism. This being the case, Rorty admits he has to acknowledge:

> When the secret police come, when the torturers violate the innocent, there is nothing to be said to them of the form "There is something within you which you are betraying. Though you embody the practices of a totalitarian society, which will endure forever, there is something beyond those practices which condemns you."[20]

For Rorty, the truth of moral values depends simply upon their existence and acceptance within society. This view has been severely criticized as adopting an uncritical approach concerning prevailing social conventions. As Richard Bernstein points out, Rorty appears to have done little more than reify social practices, and treat these as being synonymous with truth, goodness, or justice.

All these concerns point to the need for a transcendent ground of morality. Otherwise, we are trapped in the shifting sands of influential power groups, with morality being redefined to suit the needs of those with influence. Apologetic arguments that appeal to morality tend to fall into two slightly different groups: those that appeal to the intellectual advantage of belief in God as a foundation for moral values, and those that appeal to the practical value of belief in God in securing the stability of moral values. Both hold it is reasonable to believe God exists, in that this belief offers what seems to be the best explanation for the existence, nature, and our knowledge of objective moral truths.

For example, in *Mere Christianity*, C. S. Lewis sets out why our notions of right and wrong can act as "clues to the meaning of the universe." His moral argument for the existence of God could be summarized like this:

> Premise 1: Everyone believes that there are objective moral truths. We cannot conduct moral debates without them.
>
> Premise 2: Objective moral truths are quite unlike "laws of nature" or "natural" facts. The former are about what we "ought" to do; the latter about what we observe in the world around us.
>
> Conclusion: The best explanation of our deep intuition of the existence of objective moral truths is that there is an intelligence behind or beyond nature that implants the knowledge of right and wrong in us and acts as the foundation for the objectivity of our moral judgments.[21]

Lewis's approach, like most statements of this argument, does not have the logical force of a deductive proof. It is much better understood as a further demonstration of the intrinsic reasonableness of the Christian faith. If there is a God, this provides a firmer foundation for the deep human instinct and intuition that objective moral values exist, and provides a defense of morality against more irresponsible statements of ethical relativism. God, for Lewis, is made known through our deep moral and aesthetic intuitions:

> If there was a controlling power outside the universe, it could not show itself to us as one of the facts inside the universe—no more than the architect of a house could actually be a wall or staircase or fireplace in that house. The only way in which we could expect it to show itself would be inside ourselves as an influence or a command trying to get us to behave in a certain way. And that is just what we do find inside ourselves.[22]

Belief in God is thus convincing and plausible on the one hand, and useful on the other. It doesn't *make* us good; but it opens the door to that possibility. As Lewis points out, "no justification of virtue will enable a man to be virtuous."[23] If we are to be good, we must first know what "good" is—and then be enabled to achieve it. And that, as Lewis rightly saw, depends upon a realization of our true situation and its limitations. We still need to be healed and helped if we are to be good. Yet discovering and experiencing the grace of God is an important step along the road to true morality.

So how can we use such approaches apologetically? It is important to note that apologetics can work either by developing arguments in favor of Christian belief or by developing critiques of non-Christian approaches. Francis Schaeffer once famously declared that all non-Christian perspectives ultimately turn out to be incoherent and contradictory. While this claim may be slightly overstated, there is nevertheless an important element of truth in it. The "argument from morality" is an excellent example of this. Can the idea of stable, objective moral values be sustained without belief in a transcendent reality such as the Christian God?

It is clear that the argument from morality can be used effectively to reinforce the basic claim that the Christian faith makes sense of things, extending the approaches noted earlier. But the approach is perhaps better used as a critique of non-theistic worldviews. For example, can atheism defend the idea of moral truths?

At a popular level, atheist apologists react with anger to such probing of their ideas, suggesting that it amounts to suggesting they are immoral. It doesn't. It's not denying that atheists have moral values. It's asking how these values are *justified*. For example, consider a fundamental criticism of Rorty's approach to ethics—that Rorty seems incapable of offering a criterion that stands *above* human practice, by which the latter can be judged.[24] Atheist philosopher Iris Murdoch argued that a transcendent notion of goodness was essential if defensible human notions of "right" and "justice" were to be maintained. If she's right, our longing for justice is itself a deep clue to the meaning of things.

Clue 5: Desire—A Homing Instinct for God

Many arguments for the existence of God involve an appeal primarily to reason. Others involve an appeal to experience, finding their plausibility within the human heart as much as in human reason. As

Pascal once famously commented, "The heart has its reasons, which reason does not understand." The best known of these arguments is the "argument from desire." Although this takes various forms, it is most commonly framed in terms of a deep human awareness of a longing for something that is not possessed but whose attraction is felt. Christian apologists argue that this deep sense of yearning for something transcendent is ultimately grounded in the fact that we are created to fellowship with God, and will not be fulfilled until we do so.

One of the most rigorous theological treatments of this topic is found in the writings of Augustine of Hippo. For Augustine, God has created human beings and placed them at the height of the created order, so that they might fulfill their purposes through relating to God as their creator and savior. Without such a relationship, humanity cannot be what it is meant to be. As Augustine put it in a famous prayer to God: "You have made us for yourself, and our hearts are restless until they finds their rest in you."[25]

The two most significant apologetic applications of this approach were developed by Blaise Pascal (1623–62) and C. S. Lewis (1898–1963). Pascal argues that the human experience of emptiness and yearning is a pointer to the true destiny of humanity. It illuminates human nature and discloses our ultimate goal—which, for Pascal, is God.

> What else does this longing and helplessness show us, other than that there was once in each person a true happiness, of which all that now remains is the empty print and trace?[26]

Nothing other than God is able to fill this "abyss"—a profound, God-shaped gap within human nature, implanted by God as a means of drawing people back to him.

> This infinite abyss can only be filled with something that is infinite and unchanging—in other words, by God himself. God alone is our true good.[27]

Pascal's idea here is often expressed in terms of a "God-shaped gap" or "God-shaped vacuum" within human nature. Although Pascal did not actually use these phrases, they are a good summary of his approach. Pascal argues that the Christian faith offers a framework that interprets the widespread human experience of "longing and helplessness." This interpretation has two elements: first, it makes sense of the experience; second, having identified what it is pointing to, it allows this human experience to be transformed.

C. S. Lewis develops a related approach that has an obvious importance for Christian apologetics.[28] Lewis acknowledges the importance of frustrated aspirations for many: "There was something we grasped at, in that first moment of longing, which just fades away in the reality." So how is this to be interpreted? Lewis notes two possibilities he regards as flawed: first, to assume that this frustration arises from looking in the wrong places; second, to conclude that further searching will only result in repeated disappointment, so any attempt to find something better than the world can offer is a mistake. There is, Lewis argues, a third approach—to recognize that these earthly longings are "only a kind of copy, or echo, or mirage" of our true homeland.

Lewis then develops what some might call an "argument from desire," which could be formalized as follows:

1. Every natural desire has a corresponding object, and is satisfied only when this is attained or experienced.
2. There is a natural desire for transcendent fulfillment, which cannot be attained or experienced by or through anything in the present world.
3. This natural desire for transcendent fulfillment can therefore only be fulfilled beyond the present world, in a world toward which the present order of things points.[29]

Now this is not really an argument for the existence of God, in the strict sense of the term. For a start, we would need to expand Lewis's point to include the Christian declaration that God either is, or is an essential condition for, the satisfaction of the natural human desire for transcendent fulfillment. Yet even then, this is not an argument to be understood as a deduction of God's existence.

Yet Lewis saw this line of thought as demonstrating the correlation of faith with experience, exploring the "empirical adequacy" of the Christian way of seeing reality with what we experience within ourselves. It is not deductive, but—to use Peirce's term once again—abductive. Lewis clearly believes the Christian faith casts light upon the realities of our subjective experience. Augustine of Hippo wove the central themes of the Christian doctrines of creation and redemption into a prayer: "You have made us for yourself, and our hearts are restless until they find their rest in you."[30] Lewis reaffirms this notion, and seeks to ground it in the world of human experience, which he believes it illuminates.

Lewis thus contends that Christian apologetics must engage with this fundamental human experience of "longing" for something of ultimate significance. The Christian faith interprets this as a clue toward grasping the true goal of human nature. Just as physical hunger points to a real human need that can be met through food, so this spiritual hunger corresponds to a real need that can be met through God. Lewis argues that most people are aware of a deep sense of longing within them that cannot be satisfied by anything transient or created: "If I find in myself a desire which no experience in this world can satisfy, the most probable explanation is that I was made for another world."[31]

Now this *proves* nothing. After all, I might have a deep desire to meet a golden unicorn. But that doesn't mean unicorns—whether golden or not—actually exist. That's not Lewis's point. Christianity, he points out, tells us that this sense of longing for God is exactly what we should expect, since we are created to relate to God. It fits in with a Christian way of thinking, thus providing indirect confirmation of its reliability. There is a strong resonance between theory and observation—between the theological framework and the realities of our personal experience.

So how can this approach be developed and applied apologetically? Its essential feature is an appeal to human experience—to the subjective world of feelings, rather than to objective analysis of the natural world. Yet these subjective experiences are important to people, not least because people feel they are deeply significant. Not everyone recognizes this kind of experience when it is described; nevertheless, its presence is sufficiently widespread to act as the basis for an important apologetic strategy. Three points need to be made about this approach.

1. This approach *connects* with a shared human experience. It engages with something that resonates with many people, offering an explanation of a feeling that many have had and wondered what it meant.

2. This experience is *interpreted*. It is not a random or meaning-less experience, but something pointing to something that lies beyond it. What some might regard as a pointless phenomenon thus becomes a signpost to significance.

3. The experience is declared to be a *gateway to God*. Only God can bring about the transformation of human experi-ence. Only God can fill what Pascal called the "abyss" within human nature. This interpretation of human experience is not opportunistic or arbitrary, but rather is rigorously grounded in a theological understanding of human nature and destiny.

This "argument from desire" is not a rigorous, logical "proof" of God's existence; it works at a much deeper level. It may lack logical force, but it possesses existential depth. It is about the capac-ity of the Christian faith to address the depths of human experi-ence—the things that we feel really matter. It builds on the sense of restlessness and dissatisfaction within human nature and shows how this is a clue to our true nature and destiny. As Lewis argued, if nothing in this world is able to satisfy these deep longings and yearnings, maybe we must learn to accept that our true home is in another world. To use an image from Renaissance poet Francis Quarles (1592–1644), our soul is like an iron needle drawn to the magnetic pole of God. God can no more be eliminated from human life than our yearning for justice or our deep desire to make this world a better place. We have a homing instinct precisely because there is a home for us to return to. That's one of the great themes of the New Testament.

This desire is an important point for reflection on the nature of western society. Political philosopher Charles Taylor concluded his recent extended analysis of the emergence of a "secular age" with an assertion that religion will not and cannot disappear be-cause of the distinctive characteristics of human nature—above all, what French philosopher Chantal Milon-Delsol calls a "desire for eternity."[32] There is something about human nature that makes us want to reach beyond rational and empirical limits, questing for meaning and significance.

A further point needs to be made here: the Christian idea of humanity bearing the image of God has important implications for the role of the imagination. Both Lewis and Tolkien emphasize how our imaginations open up worlds that reflect hints of our true identity and destiny. Often, we dream of beautiful worlds not because we want to escape from this world, but because something deep within us causes us to long for this kind of reality. As we shall see in what follows, this also has relevance for Christian apologetics.

Clue 6: Beauty—The Splendor of the Natural World

Many find themselves deeply moved by a scene of natural beauty—for example, a great mountain range, a glorious sunset, or wooded valleys. So how can we help someone move from a love of what God has created to a love of God the creator? Perhaps the first and most obvious point is that we need to help people see the world in a different way—as a signpost, not a destination. The beauty of the world is a pointer toward the greater beauty of God, which it reflects as the moon reflects the greater light of the sun, or as a beautiful diamond scintillates as it catches the beams of the sun.

This is a leading theme of the great American theologian Jonathan Edwards, who provides a rigorous theological foundation for an apologetic approach based on an appeal to the beauty of nature. For Edwards, God desires his beauty to be known and enjoyed by his creatures and thus chooses to communicate that beauty through the created order so all might see, acknowledge, and respond to it.[33] Nature is *meant* to disclose the beauty of God, functioning as a school of desire in which humanity may learn how to perceive God's glory and respond in faith and awe.

Yet we need to think more about the notion of beauty. To appreciate a rational argument, I need to think it through; it's not immediately obvious. Beauty, however, is quite different. Beauty is something we appreciate *immediately*. When we see a beautiful scene, person, or work of art, we instantly know there is something special about it. We do not need to be persuaded that something or someone is beautiful; something deep within us seems to tell us. An apologetic based on beauty is not initially about argument; it is about appreciation. The arguments begin when we ask what the beauty of nature points to—if anything.

Maybe our realization of the beauty of nature means nothing whatsoever. It could all be an accident, something arbitrary and meaningless. Then again, it might be what C. S. Lewis terms a "clue to the meaning of the universe."[34] In a variant of the argument from desire, Lewis contends that our longing for beauty will be utterly frustrated if we think we will find true beauty in anything that is created or finite. It's like looking for the pot of gold at the end of the rainbow. For Lewis, things in this world are signs—they point to where we may find what they signify, but they don't deliver true beauty themselves. If we think they will, we will end up miserable and confused.

The human quest for true beauty is, for Lewis, an important point of contact for the Christian gospel. It is a central theme of arguably his most important shorter work, the 1941 sermon "The Weight of Glory".[35] Lewis argues that we possess an instinct for transcendence, stimulated by beauty—"a desire for our own far-off country, which we find in ourselves even now."[36] For Lewis, beauty evokes an ideal that is more real than anything we encounter in this transitory world. It stirs up a sense of longing—such as we considered in the previous section of this chapter—for a half-remembered realm from which we are presently exiled. It is a desire "for something that has never actually appeared in our experience," yet is constantly suggested and intimated by our experience.[37]

The human quest for beauty is thus really a quest for the *source* of that beauty, which is mediated through the things of this world, not contained within them. Those things "in which we thought the beauty was located will betray us if we trust to them: it was not *in* them, it only came *through* them, and what came through them was longing."[38] That is why that quest ends in frustration or despair. "Beauty has smiled, but not to welcome us."[39] We catch a glimpse of that indescribable something of which beauty is the messenger, mistakenly believing it to be the message itself.

Lewis thus argues that we must learn to see nature as a signpost to the greater beauty of God. The "authoritative imagery" of the Christian tradition addresses the longing we *know* and *experience*, while promising to reveal what presently lies concealed—"what we do not yet know and need to know."[40] It interprets this quest for beauty as "a longing to be reunited with something in the universe from which we now feel cut off, to be on the inside of some door which we have always seen from the outside."[41] This experience of desiring beauty is really a summons "to pass in and through Nature, beyond her, into that splendor which she fitfully reflects."[42]

Nature thus turns out to be "the first sketch ... only the image, the symbol," of that greater reality to which it points. Nature is thus a "good image of what we really desire," which people mistake for the thing itself.[43] Beauty reveals truth by pointing to a realm beyond the visible world of particulars. It allows us to see beyond a door that is presently closed, to anticipate opening it and crossing its threshold.

> We cannot mingle with the splendors we see. But all the leaves of the New Testament are rustling with the rumor that it will *not* always be so. Some day, God willing, we shall get *in*.[44]

Similar ideas are found in writers such as Jonathan Edwards and Hans Urs von Balthasar. All beauty in the created order, both in the heavens and on the earth, is derived from the radiance of Jesus Christ, who is the image of the beautiful God, the source of all beauty.

So how do we use an appeal to beauty in our apologetics? For Lewis, the answer is simple: beauty bypasses rational analysis, appealing to something far deeper within us. A lawyer friend of mine and his girlfriend decided to get married. They went to a jeweler to buy the ring. They had a checklist of things they wanted—what sort of setting, what type of precious stone, and so on. Then they saw a ring they both fell in love with. It didn't fit their checklist. But they knew it was right, and went home rejoicing at their purchase.

The apologetic implications of this story are not difficult to discern! Sometimes the important thing is to allow the gospel to persuade people by itself. The merchant in the parable who recognized the beauty and value of the "pearl of great price" did not need to be persuaded of its true worth (Matt. 13:45–46). The pearl persuaded him by itself. We may help people to grasp the gospel's beauty, just as a jeweler might hold a diamond up to the light so its facets scintillate and its beauty can be appreciated. But the beauty is already there; the jeweler is simply showing it off to its best advantage.

Clue 7: Relationality—God as a Person

The Genesis creation accounts emphasize the goodness of God's creation. Yet there is one point at which God judges that a change needs to be made. It is not good that Adam is alone (Gen. 2:18). We see here a recognition of the *relationality* of human beings. We have been created to exist in relationship—with one another, and with God. The biblical depiction of the paradisiacal Garden of Eden represents Adam and Eve in harmony with each other and with God. To be authentically human is to exist in relationship—as we are meant to.

The fundamental need of human beings to exist in relationship has been long recognized. When Aristotle, one of the great philosophers of the classic age, famously declared that human beings were "political animals," he really meant they had a natural tendency to live together in communities—such as the classic Greek city-state. Yet for most people, the most important way of understanding our need for relationships is not expressed in political terms, but in the intensely personal language of *love*.

"The supreme happiness in life is the conviction that we are loved." Thus wrote famous French playwright Victor Hugo (1802–85). Knowing we are loved gives us the secure base we need to get on with our lives. We need to know that we matter to someone. Vast numbers of dull academic articles and trashy romantic novels have been written on the same basic theme: Why is it that rich and powerful people are so *unhappy*? Love is what really matters to people, not wealth or power. We can't live without meaningful personal relationships.

Many stories could be told to illustrate this point. My favorite concerns American philosopher Paul Elmer More (1864–1937). As a younger man, More was fascinated by Plato's notion of the Ideal—the reality that lies behind any appearance on earth. Yet the more he reflected on Plato's "world of Ideals," the less it appealed to him. It seemed bleak and sterile, lacking a capacity to *relate* to people. For More, Plato's was a chilly and impersonal world, in which no words are spoken and the tenderness of love is unknown. Yet Christianity speaks of God entering into our history and allows us to abandon the cold and unfeeling world of ideals in favor of a world charged with the thrilling personal presence of God. That difference matters profoundly. No wonder More became a Christian later in life.[45] No human being can rest satisfied with an abstract and impersonal world. We need to relate to others—including God.

Christianity is a fundamentally *relational* faith. We must never think of the gospel in purely rational terms—for example, believing that there is a God, as if faith was simply assent to a list of propositions. There is indeed a definite content to faith, in that we believe certain things to be true about God and about ourselves. But there is far more to faith than this. We must never forget that the core biblical idea of faith is fundamentally about trusting a God who shows himself to be worthy of that trust, in word and deed. The ideas of faith, hope, and love are deeply interconnected. We trust in a God who loves us and gives us hope for the future.

The relational aspects of faith can be seen in countless biblical passages. Think, for example, of the call of Abraham (Gen. 15, 17). At the heart of these biblical narratives lies the idea of human trust in divine promises. It is about the forging of a trusting, obedient relationship between Abraham and God. Or consider the calling of the first disciples by the shores of the Sea of Galilee (Mark 1:16–20). Jesus invites the fishermen to follow him—to enter into a relationship with him.

Throughout Scripture, God is understood to be a *person*—not an impersonal force—who loves us and wants to enter into a relationship with us. The language we use to refer to our relationship with God is analogous to the terms we use to refer to our relationships with other people, such as "love" and "commitment." For example, Paul uses the term "reconciliation" in his letters to refer to both the restoration of the relationship of estranged people and the restoration of fellowship between God and humanity through Christ.

The essential apologetic point made here rests on solid theological foundations: we have been created in order that we might relate to God, and we are restless and unfulfilled until we do so. We have been created "in the image of God" (Gen. 1:27), so there is an inbuilt correspondence—not identity!—between God and each of us. We are defined as human beings by our God-given capacity to relate to God as our creator and redeemer. It is in coming to faith in God that we become whom we are meant to be. Authentic existence is not to be had through possessions, status, or power, but through embracing and being embraced by the loving and living God.

This immediately links up with a theme we have already explored earlier in the chapter—namely, the argument from desire. Yet this is a desire for a *person*, not for an impersonal object or force. God is one whom we *know*, not just *know about*. There is indeed a "God-shaped gap" within us, which points to our need to relate to God so we may become what God wants us to be. Without God, we are empty and unfulfilled.

Clue 8: Eternity—The Intuition of Hope

Some biblical passages are difficult to translate into English on account of the richness and complexity of the original Hebrew or Greek. As they say, things get lost in translation. The third chapter of Ecclesiastes takes the form of an extended meditation on our place in the flow of time. One of its sections has proved particularly difficult to render in English. In creating humanity, God has "put a sense of past and future into their minds" (Eccles. 3:11). Yet this phrase does not quite convey the sense of the passage. Perhaps another way of translating this would be to say God has "planted eternity in their hearts." We already possess a sense of the brevity of human life, and a deep-seated intuition that there is more to reality than the brief slice of time and space allocated to us. Our transient existence in this world suggests the possibility of something greater and better beyond it. We have a hunch we were made for more than just this life. But what? And how do we take hold of it?

This sense that our true destiny lies beyond this transient world is heightened by several factors. One is a deep intuition that this is not where we belong. Augustine of Hippo, writing in the fifth century, spoke of the haunting memory of paradise, which we can never shake off. Even in the midst of a busy life, we are reminded of another world, another way of existing. Voices seem to call to us from the ends of the earth, pointing to something deeper and better than anything we presently possess or know. As poet Matthew Arnold (1822–88) put it in his poem *The Buried Life*, written at the height of the Victorian age:

> But often, in the world's most crowded streets
> But often, in the din of strife
> There rises an unspeakable desire
> After the knowledge of our buried life.

The memory of the garden of Eden seems imprinted on our souls, rising to challenge and refresh us when we lose sight of our true identity and goal.

A similar idea was expressed in 1969 by American musician Joni Mitchell (b. 1943) in her famous song "Woodstock." We are, she declared, "made of stardust." Yet this does not mean we are reduced to our material components—as if we are defined by the fact that we are made up of the chemical elements of the universe. There is something different about us, something that makes us stand out. We need to recover our sense of identity and purpose. How? Mitchell's answer is as dramatic as it is powerful: "We've got to get ourselves back to the garden."

This notion of hope is deeply embedded within western culture. In her recent study of cultural attitudes toward heaven, journalist Lisa Miller noted individuals and societies seemed to be hardwired to believe in "a place that embodies the best of everything—but beyond the best . . . what's most beautiful, most loving, most just, and most true."[46] This might, of course, be nothing more than a delusion, a piece of wishful thinking that shields us from the darker realities of life. Or it might represent a clue to our true identity and significance. For Miller, we have a "radical hope" that keeps us going, even in situations of despair. It is easy to see how this can be correlated with the Christian vision of hope, grounded in the resurrection of Jesus Christ and the firm and confident expectation of finally being in the presence of God in the New Jerusalem.

The apologist's task is to connect with this deep intuition of the human heart and show how the Christian faith makes sense of it and offers a real hope that is firmly grounded in the reality of God. We begin with that sense of hope and ask to what it might point. We then explain the nature of Christian hope, and show how it brings this fundamental intuition of the human heart to fulfillment. Maybe God has planted the idea of eternity in our hearts as a clue to the true meaning of the universe. Maybe we are meant to think such thoughts and experience such longings because that's the way God created us.

This is not really a *logical* argument. It's much more a demonstration of the capacity of the Christian faith to make sense of the human situation and show us how our intuitions can find true fulfillment in Christ. It is about interpretation of the human situation as preparation for its redirection and transformation.

Weaving Clues Together: In Search of a Pattern

We noted earlier the comment of American poet Edna St. Vincent Millay, who wrote of "a meteoric shower of facts" raining from the sky. These facts, she suggested, are like threads that need to be woven into a tapestry, clues that need to be assembled to disclose the big picture. As Millay pointed out, when confronted with such a shower of facts, we need a "loom to weave it into fabric." What is the pattern behind the facts?

In this chapter we have considered eight clues to the meaning of the universe. Each of these is significant in its own right; their true importance, however, lies in the overall pattern they disclose. They are like threads in the tapestry of faith. Christian theology is the loom that allows them to be woven together so their true significance can be appreciated and understood. While each thread may be appreciated individually, they have a greater significance when they are woven together to form a coherent and beautiful pattern.

Some of these clues concern our observations of the world around us; some of them concern our world of inner experience. Yet whether we consider the thoughts of our minds or the longings of our hearts, we discover that the Christian faith is able to make sense of these clues and position them within the greater picture of reality as disclosed by the gospel. This capacity to connect with our experience and make sense of it is a surefire indication of both the rational truth and existential adequacy of the Christian faith.

Philosopher John Cottingham recently offered a fine account of why the Christian belief in God is so intellectually robust and spiritually satisfying:

> It provides a *framework* that frees us from the threats of contingency and futility that lurk beneath the surface of supposedly self-sufficient and autonomous secular ethics. It offers us not a proof but a hope that the "cave" of our human world (to use Plato's image) is not utterly sealed and closed, but that our flickering moral intimations reflect the ultimate source of all goodness.[47]

In much the same way, Cottingham argues, our aesthetic intimations reflect and point to the ultimate source of beauty. The gospel makes sense of these "clues," while at the same time redirecting them toward their true origin and goal.

The approach developed here can be explored more rigorously by using the theological framework developed in the opening chapters of *Institutes of the Christian Religion* by John Calvin (1509–64).[48] Calvin argues here that we possess intuitions or perceptions of God, grounded either through reflection on the world around us or an inner awareness of God's presence within us. He treats these as valid, yet incomplete. They are pointers to something greater. Calvin then argues that a full knowledge of God, grounded in divine revelation, is able to engage these perceptions to allow them to be understood properly and to allow them to be reinterpreted, redirected, and hence ultimately fulfilled by redemption through Christ.

The apologetic approach adopted in this chapter is thus to identify clues about the meaning of the universe—whether drawn from our observations of the world around us or from the deepest subjective feelings and yearnings of humanity. Taken together, these are significant pointers to the capacity of the Christian faith to make sense of life. Yet these clues also need to be appreciated and applied *individually*. Each of these clues is important in its own right and sparks its own apologetic strategy and approach. Let me explain what I mean.

Let's take just one of these clues, the ordering of the universe, and see how we can work its angles apologetically. How might we explore this clue and help people to grasp its possible significance? How can we appeal to the regularity and ordering of the universe, and help people to see how this points to its origin in God? Let me offer an example, which is part of a lecture I gave for the British Broadcasting Corporation, transmitted in March 2010. In this short lecture, I worked the angles of this "clue," opening with an incident from classical antiquity:

> The story is told of the ancient Greek philosopher Aristippus, who found himself washed up on the shore of the island of Rhodes. He knew nothing of the place. Was it inhabited? As he walked along the shore, he found some geometric patterns marked out in the sand. "There is hope!" he declared. "There must be people here!" Aristippus had seen features of the natural landscape which seemed to him to point to human intelligence. The patterns stood out as having been designed and drawn by people like himself. He was not on his own.

I then noted how the universe seemed to show regular patterns of its own—such as fine-tuning. And just as Aristippus reasoned from intelligent designs on the Rhodian shore to the existence of intelligent agents who designed them, I argued from the order of the world to the existence of a creator. Here is how the lecture ended, as I reflected on possible explanations for the strange ordering and patterns of our universe:

> One such answer is that we find our true identity and meaning through coming to know God. This is now the answer—or, at least, part of the answer—that I myself would give. It is not one that I always adopted. While I was a student at Oxford many years ago, it gradually came to capture my thoughts and imagination.
>
> It is an answer that continues to thrill and excite me. For me, discovering God was like finding a lens that helped me see things more clearly. Faith offers a bigger picture of reality. It doesn't just make sense *to* me; it makes sense *of* me as well. C. S. Lewis once wrote: "I believe in Christianity as I believe that the sun has risen; not just because I see it, but because by it, I see everything else." I do not find that believing in God contradicts science, but rather

that it gives me an intellectual and moral framework within which the successes of science may be celebrated and understood, and its limits appreciated.

Let me end with a reflection of Sir Isaac Newton, one of the most significant contributors to the scientific revolution of the seventeenth century. Newton's scientific and mathematical breakthroughs—such as his discovery of the laws of planetary motion, and his theory of optics—placed him at the forefront of new scientific understandings of nature. Yet for Newton, what could be seen of nature was as a pointer to something deeper, lying beyond it, signposted by what could be seen. As he wrote towards the end of his life: "I seem to have been only like a boy playing on the sea-shore, and diverting myself in now and then finding a smoother pebble or a prettier shell than ordinary, whilst the great ocean of truth lay all undiscovered before me." That ocean is still there, its unplumbed depths inviting us to go deeper and go further.

Notice how I developed an approach that is *apologetic*, not *evangelistic*. I did not set out to convert, but to entice, intrigue, interest, and ultimately *convince*. What is the best explanation of this clue? And what are its implications for human existence? We can all agree that much more needs to be said. But in many ways, apologetics can be thought of as getting a serious conversation under way by getting our audience—whether it is a single person or a roomful of people—interested and intrigued by the deep questions we are exploring. Apologetics begins the conversation; evangelism brings it to its conclusion.

Moving On

In this chapter, we have considered "clues" to the meaning of the universe that lie scattered around us. Many of them will be known to our audiences. Yet they may not have worked out what these clues mean. Our task as apologists is to connect all of these dots, placing the clues in their proper context.

Yet there is another point that needs to be noted here. In an earlier chapter, we emphasized the importance of our audiences. Each audience is different! Some may value rational argument.

Others, however, may value an approach that works at a deeper level—for example, the appeal to beauty, or a sense of human longing for something of ultimate significance. We are not limited to arguments appealing to human reason, but are able to engage every aspect of human nature—including human imagination, feelings, and intuition. In the following chapter, we shall consider a series of gateways to faith, assessing their significance and how each might best be used.

For Further Reading

Craig, William Lane. "In Defense of Theistic Arguments." In *The Future of Atheism*, edited by Robert B. Stewart, 67–96. Minneapolis: Fortress Press, 2008.

Dubay, Thomas. *The Evidential Power of Beauty: Science and Theology Meet.* San Francisco: Ignatius Press, 1999.

Evans, C. Stephen. *Natural Signs and Knowledge of God: A New Look at Theistic Arguments.* Oxford: Oxford University Press, 2010.

Feingold, Lawrence. *The Natural Desire to See God According to St. Thomas and His Interpreters.* Rome: Apollinare Studi, 2001.

Haldane, John. "Philosophy, the Restless Heart, and the Meaning of Theism." *Ratio* 19 (2006): 421–40.

Hart, David Bentley. *The Beauty of the Infinite: The Aesthetics of Christian Truth.* Grand Rapids: Eerdmans, 2003.

Keller, Timothy J. *Counterfeit Gods: The Empty Promises of Money, Sex, and Power, and the Only Hope That Matters* (New York: Dutton, 2009).

McGrath, Alister E. *Surprised by Meaning: Science, Faith, and How We Make Sense of Things.* Louisville: Westminster John Knox, 2011.

Peters, James R. *The Logic of the Heart: Augustine, Pascal, and the Rationality of Faith.* Grand Rapids: Baker Academic, 2009.

Plantinga, Alvin. *Warranted Christian Belief.* Oxford: Oxford University Press, 2000.

Polkinghorne, John. *Science and Creation: The Search for Understanding.* London: SPCK, 1988.

Spitzer, Robert J. *New Proofs for the Existence of God: Contributions of Contemporary Physics and Philosophy.* Grand Rapids: Eerdmans, 2010.

Swinburne, Richard. *The Existence of God*. 2nd ed. Oxford: Clarendon Press, 2004.

Warren, Rick. *The Purpose Driven Life: What on Earth Am I Here For?* Grand Rapids: Zondervan, 2002.

Wolterstorff, Nicholas. "The Migration of the Theistic Arguments: From Natural Theology to Evidentialist Apologetics." In *Rationality, Religious Belief, and Moral Commitment*, edited by Robert Audi and William J. Wainwright, 38–80. Ithaca, NY: Cornell University Press, 1986.

7

Gateways for Apologetics

OPENING THE DOOR TO FAITH

pologetics can be likened to drawing curtains to one side so people can catch a glimpse of what lies beyond, or holding a diamond up to the light and allowing its facets to scintillate and sparkle in the sunlight. It's about establishing *gateways* for faith—whether we think of this as opening doors, drawing curtains aside, turning on a light so people can see more clearly, or using a lens that brings things into sharper focus. The key themes are those of allowing people to see things clearly, perhaps for the first time; to discover insights that had previously eluded them; and to suddenly realize why people might find the Christian faith so intellectually persuasive and imaginatively compelling.

Apologetics is about building bridges, allowing people to cross from the world they already know to one they need to discover. It is about helping people to find doors they may never have known about, allowing them to see and enter a world that exceeds anything they could have imagined. Apologetics opens eyes and opens doors, establishing gateways for the Christian faith. So what gateways are we talking about?

Until quite recently, the dominant trend in apologetics was to use arguments in the reasoned defense of the Christian faith. Yet this was largely a response to a strongly rationalist culture, which saw conformity to reason as a criterion of truth. The use of arguments, as we shall see, remains an integral part of Christian apologetics and must never be marginalized. However, the waning of rationalism in western culture has made this less important than it once was, and created a context in which other aspects of the Christian faith need to be recognized—above all, its powerful imaginative, moral, and aesthetic appeal. Older Christian writers, particularly those who lived during the Middle Ages and Renaissance, placed a high value on biblical stories and images in teaching the faithful; the rise of modernity caused these both to be devalued, just as the later rise of postmodernity has led to a rediscovery of their power.

The recent growth of postmodernity has led to a new emphasis on the importance of *story* and *image*, both of which make a significant appeal to the human imagination. Anyone familiar with the history of Christian apologetics quickly realizes that both of these were used extensively as gateways to faith by earlier generations of apologists, particularly during the Renaissance. We need to retrieve such older approaches to apologetics as we develop a balanced approach to the commendation and defense of the Christian faith in our shifting cultural context.

We need to adapt our apologetics to our audiences, realizing there are several gateways of connection between the gospel and the human soul. The New Testament itself is obviously concerned with linking the gospel to the conceptual and experiential world of multiple audiences. If the soul thirsts for God "like a parched land" (Ps. 143:6), how can it be irrigated? Our task is to identify the possible channels through which the living water of the gospel can refresh and transform the human soul, and then use these channels faithfully and effectively. In this chapter, I shall use the image of a gateway to help us reflect on these varied approaches.

Gateways and Apologetics: Some Reflections

One of the most important images used by medieval theologians to discuss how the human soul is transformed by God's grace is that of the sun and the shutter. A good example is found in the writings of Alan of Lille (d. 1203), who compares the human soul to a cold, dark room. When the shutters are thrown open, sunlight pours into the room, lighting and warming it. We open the shutters; the sun illuminates and heats the room. The opening of the shutters doesn't really cause the room to become warm and light. It just removes a barrier to a force that is able to achieve this. The real cause of the change is the sun. We simply allow the light and heat of the sun to enter the room by removing an obstacle to their entry.

This image helps us grasp the theological point that we do not *cause* conversion. Alan argues that we are the ones who must throw open the shutters of our minds, so God's grace can get to work in our lives. We simply remove an obstacle to God's grace; it is divine grace that causes the renewal of our souls. Yet the image is also important apologetically. It reminds us that God is the one who converts people, while at the same time reaffirming we can aid this process by helping remove barriers and obstacles to the grace of God.

A gateway is a means by which our eyes are opened to the reality of our own situation and the ability of the gospel to transform it. To understand this important point, imagine that you are seriously ill; you have blood poisoning and will die within hours unless you gain access to the drugs that will cure you. But you don't really understand what is wrong with you. Nor do you know a cure is available. Try thinking yourself into that situation. Now consider the following approaches, each of which is a gateway to your transformation:

1. A friend is a medical doctor. She tells you your symptoms are those of blood poisoning. She explains this will be fatal unless it is treated. She gives you the names of several drugs that will cure you, and tells you where to get them and how to administer them.
2. Another friend tells you he had symptoms just like yours. He became very seriously ill. However, he tells you that someone told him about a certain drug, which saved his life. He suggests you try the same thing. In other words, he tells you his own story, which intersects with your story at this important point.

The first approach is an evidence-based argument; the second approach is story, based on a personal experience the storyteller considers relevant to your situation. Each approach is very different from the other. Yet each acts as a gateway. How?

First, they help you to see things in a different way—the way things really are. Second, they allow you to appreciate what can be done to transform things. Third, they encourage you to make that critical step—to get the drug, take it, and become better.

What cured you was the drug. But without realizing your true situation—that you *needed* that drug—you would not have been cured. God's grace is the drug; now that you are cured, you can help people see their need for that grace and can testify to its power. God converts and brings to faith; you are nevertheless a small (but real!) part of this process of healing. What you say can thus be a gateway allowing people to see things in a different way and begin to imagine a new way of thinking and living.

So what are these gateways for Christian apologetics? In this chapter, we shall explore some of the possibilities open to apologists. We begin with what is possibly the simplest way of doing apologetics: explaining what Christianity really is.

Gateway 1: Explanation

The best defense of Christianity is its explanation. In other words, if you want to defend or commend Christianity, it is best to begin by telling people what it is really all about. Many people have misconceptions of Christianity that get in the way of their coming to faith. One of the best examples of this is provided by the great theologian Augustine of Hippo, who came to faith after a long time of wandering in the philosophical wastelands.[1] Augustine was a talented young orator from North Africa who fell in with the Manichaeans, a sect that was severely critical of Christianity. His knowledge of Christianity came primarily from its critics and was not particularly accurate. Augustine rejected Christianity as unworthy of consideration by someone as cultured and intelligent as himself.

Augustine was ambitious, and decided to try to make his mark in the imperial capital. Leaving North Africa, he traveled to Rome. Soon after his arrival at Rome, he was offered the job of Public Orator in the major northern Italian city of Milan. Aware that this could be the beginning of a significant career in the imperial civil service, Augustine accepted with alacrity. Yet he was also aware that his political advancement would depend on his rhetorical skills. Who could help him develop as a public speaker?

After his arrival at Milan, Augustine discovered that the local Christian bishop, Ambrose, had a reputation as a splendid orator. He decided to find out whether the reputation was merited. Each Sunday, he slipped into the city's great cathedral and listened to the bishop preach. Initially, he took a purely professional interest in the sermons as pieces of splendid oratory. But gradually, their content began to take hold of him.

> I used enthusiastically to listen to him preaching to the people, not with the intention which I ought to have had, but as if testing out his oratorical skill to see whether his fluency was better or inferior than it was reported to be. . . . I was not interested in learning what he was talking about. My ears were only for his rhetorical technique. . . . Nevertheless together with the words which I was enjoying, the subject matter, in which I was unconcerned, came to make an entry into my mind. I could not separate them. While I opened my heart in noting the eloquence with which he spoke, there also entered no less the truth which he affirmed.[2]

As the story of Augustine's long journey to faith makes clear, Ambrose (whom Augustine came to regard as a kind of theological hero) removed a major barrier to faith. He disarmed the Manichaean stereotype of Christianity. After listening to Ambrose, Augustine began to realize that Christianity was far more attractive and persuasive than he had realized. A barrier to faith was removed. Although it would be some time before Augustine converted to Christianity, his encounter with Ambrose was a milestone along that road.

Among the individuals whom we encounter in our apologetic ministry, there will certainly be some who have the most astonishingly misguided and muddled ideas about what Christianity is all about. These misunderstandings—some unconsciously picked up, others deliberately propagated—need to be identified and firmly yet tactfully disarmed.

We now move on to consider what is perhaps the most familiar gateway to faith: the use of reasoned argument.

Gateway 2: Argument

Classic approaches to apologetics emphasize the importance of reason in both establishing the intellectual case for God and criticizing alternative positions. We have already considered the role of arguments in relation to defending the existence of God, including:

1. The argument from design. Here, the observation of design in the world—for example, its apparent "fine-tuning" or complexity—is held to point to its design by God (pp. 99–100).
2. The argument from origination. The realization that the universe had an origin points to it being *caused* by someone or something—an idea that naturally points to the Christian notion of God as creator of all things (pp. 96–98).
3. The argument from coherence. Here, the emphasis falls upon the ability of the Christian faith to offer an account of what we observe in both the world around us and our experiences within us (pp. 79–86, 101–3).
4. The argument from morality. The argument here is that moral values cannot be given a stable and reliable foundation without proposing that they possess a transcendent ground—for example, in a righteous God (pp. 103–8).

Other arguments could easily be added to this list. Remember, such arguments are not to be understood as "proofs" in the logically rigorous sense of the term. What such arguments make absolutely clear is that there are good reasons for believing in God—or, to put it another way, that belief in God can be *justified*, even if it cannot be absolutely *proven*.

In its rigorous sense, "proof" applies only to logic and mathematics. We can prove $2 + 2 = 4$, just as we can prove the whole is greater than the part. Nevertheless, it is important to avoid confusing "provability" with "truth." In the early twentieth century, the great mathematician Kurt Gödel famously proved that, however many rules of inference we formulate, there will still be some valid inferences not covered by them. In other words, there are some true statements that we may not be able to *show* to be true.[3] The philosophical implications of this are considerable.[4]

Argument can also be used to critique the position of alternatives to the Christian faith—such as by showing they are rationally incoherent or lack a reliable evidential foundation. For example, throughout this work we have emphasized the capacity of the Christian gospel to make sense of things. In doing so, we are not restricting the appeal of Christianity to its rational dimensions. After all, it has rich emotional, moral, imaginative, and existential aspects, all of which must be deployed to the full by the responsible apologist. Yet there is no doubt that many have been, and continue to be, drawn to the Christian faith because of its ability to make sense of things.

But what of non-Christian alternatives? How capable are rival views of making sense of things? Are they empirically adequate—in other words, how good is their theory at making sense of observation and experience? In an earlier chapter, we emphasized the apologetic importance of showing how the Christian faith is able to make sense of observation and experience. The apologist must not simply affirm the excellence of Christianity in this respect, but point out the limitations of other approaches.

This kind of tactic was developed by Francis Schaeffer (1912–84), one of the most important North American evangelical apologists of the twentieth century. Schaeffer's apologetic method emphasizes many of the points we have already made in this work. [5] For example, Schaeffer rightly draws attention to relating to a specific audience, rather than using a one-size-fits-all approach: "If we wish to communicate, then, we must take the time and the trouble to learn our hearer's use of language so that they understand what we intend to convey." [6] The apologist must listen to the intended audience to learn their language, in order to communicate with them in terms they can understand.

Schaeffer himself seems to have realized the importance of listening to the ideas, concerns, and aspirations of his audience during his time as a missionary in French-speaking Switzerland in the late 1950s and 1960s. Based in a chalet (named L'Abri, from the French word for "shelter" or "refuge") in the alpine village of Huemoz, Schaeffer acted as host to many students touring Europe, especially young Americans backpacking through Europe. He listened to their reflections on contemporary films and novels, or their take on the new philosophies of the age. How could the Bible be squared with the heady existentialist ideas of then-influential philosophers like Jean-Paul Sartre and Søren Kierkegaard? Having listened to these students talking about their ideas, Schaeffer realized he was then able to engage them on their own level and in their own language, using illustrations drawn from the world they had described to help them appreciate the plausibility of the Christian faith.

Yet Schaeffer's most significant contribution to apologetics lies in the importance he attaches to identifying points of tension within non-Christian worldviews and exploring their wider implications. Worldviews rest on certain presuppositions. If these presuppositions are human creations, lacking divine mandate and authorization, they will be incapable of corresponding to the structures of the universe, which is God's creation.

> The more logical a man who holds a non-Christian position is to his own presuppositions, the further he is from the real world; and the nearer he is to the real world, the more illogical he is to his own presuppositions.[7]

Every person, Schaeffer argues, lives with a foot in each of two worlds—the real, external world, characterized by its depth and complexity; and an internal world of thought, shaped by a longing for understanding, love, and significance. If these two worlds stand in tension with each other, an individual cannot live meaningfully. There must be a correspondence between our experience of the external world and our internal world.[8] The apologist, Schaeffer suggests, must therefore use reasoned argument to identify and expose the internal contradictions and tensions within non-Christian worldviews. These, he declares, rest on assumptions or presuppositions that are, in the end, inconsistent and incompatible with true human existence.

> Every person we speak to, whether shop girl or university student, has a set of presuppositions, whether he or she has analyzed them or not. . . . It is impossible for any non-Christian individual or group to be consistent to their system in logic or in practice. . . . A man may try to bury the tension and you may have to help him find it, but

somewhere there is a point of inconsistency. He stands in a position which he cannot pursue to the end; and this is not just an intellectual concept of tension, it is what is wrapped up in what he is as a man.[9]

The apologist must therefore help an individual to realize this "tension" and feel its intellectual and existential force. This means helping him or her first to *discover* it, and second to *appreciate* its significance. Schaeffer suggests that people shield themselves from this tension by protecting themselves with a sort of intellectual cocoon, which prevents them from experiencing the disturbing realization that their ideas simply do not correspond to the way things really are. Using an image familiar to him from winter life in Switzerland, Schaeffer likens this intellectual cocoon to the roof of an alpine shelter, designed to shield travelers from avalanches:

> It is like the great shelters built upon some mountain passes to protect vehicles from the avalanches of rock and stone which periodically tumble down the mountain. The avalanche, in the case of the non-Christian, is the real and the abnormal fallen world which surrounds him. The Christian, lovingly, must remove the shelter and allow the truth of the external world and of what man is to beat upon him.[10]

Apologetics can thus be thought of as taking the roof off such a shelter and forcing our audience to realize their way of thinking is simply not capable of withstanding an encounter with the real world outside.

So how is this method to be applied? Schaeffer himself gives an example that illustrates the approach well. He was speaking to a group of students in a room in a college at Cambridge University. As the kettle boiled to make some tea, Schaeffer was challenged by an Indian student who argued that Christianity did not make sense. Schaeffer responded by asking him about his own belief system: "Am I not correct in saying that on the basis of your system, cruelty and noncruelty are ultimately equal, that there is no intrinsic difference between them?" The student agreed. Schaeffer then narrates what happened next:

> The student in whose room we met, who had clearly understood the implications of what the Sikh had admitted, picked up his kettle of

boiling water with which he was about to make tea, and stood with it steaming over the Indian's head. The man looked up and asked him what he was doing, and he said with a cold yet gentle finality, "There is no difference between cruelty and noncruelty." Thereupon the Hindu walked out into the night.[11]

Schaeffer's approach is both versatile and rigorous, and can be applied to a number of situations. For example, consider the claims of Logical Positivism, a philosophical movement that achieved considerable influence in the English-speaking world in the 1960s. Logical Positivism declared all metaphysical statements—including statements about God—to be meaningless. The ground for doing so was a "verification principle" that restricted meaningful statements to propositions that were either true in themselves (such as "all bachelors are unmarried") or confirmed by experience (such as "there were six geese on the front lawn of Buckingham Palace at 5:23 a.m. on December 1, 1968"). Yet the application of Schaeffer's approach allows us to declare that the "verification principle" itself is meaningless, as it fails to correspond to Logical Positivism's own criterion of meaning.

Or, more simply, consider the sound bite that is often encountered on North American university campuses: "You can't be sure about anything." This is intended to subvert "big picture" views of reality, such as that of the Christian faith, by implying we ought to be skeptical about those who make confident statements about life. But it is obviously a self-referential statement, which can be undermined and subverted by simply posing a question in response: "Are you sure about that?" The assertion is defeated by its own inner logic.

We must, however, avoid thinking that our task is simply to win arguments or to set out the rational credentials of faith. The Enlightenment has had an enduring impact on western culture, especially in generating demands for proofs for beliefs. As a result, Christian apologetics has often been presented simply in terms of developing effective arguments designed to persuade people that the Christian faith is true. Yet this can all too easily end up making Christianity seem like a list of dull facts and abstract ideas. There are three difficulties with this approach.

First, this approach is not well-grounded in the Bible. Truth, especially for the Old Testament, primarily designates reliability and trustworthiness. The apologetic issue is that God is a secure base, a place of safety on which to build the life of faith. The "true God" is not merely a God who exists, but a God who may be relied upon. A rationalist notion of truth as propositional correctness can too easily displace the biblical idea of truth as a relational concept.

Second, the appeal of the Christian faith cannot be limited to the rationality of its beliefs. As the writings of C. S. Lewis indicate, Christianity also makes a powerful appeal to the imagination. As a young man, Lewis found himself yearning for a world of passion, beauty, and meaning he had come to believe did not and could not exist: "Nearly all that I loved I believed to be imaginary; nearly all that I believed to be real I thought grim and meaningless."[12] His imagination told him there was a better world; his reason told him that this was nonsense. He therefore believed he had no option other than to confront the bleakness of a senseless world and his pointless existence.

In the end, Lewis discovered the rational force of the Christian faith. Yet his attraction to the gospel was based on his perception that it offered meaning, rather than propositional correctness. As Lewis later commented, "Reason is the natural organ of truth; but imagination is the organ of meaning."[13] Others locate the appeal of the Christian faith in the beauty of its worship, its capacity to engage the human emotions, or its ethical outcomes.

Third, this rationalist approach is deeply embedded in a modernist worldview. Yet throughout most of western culture today, modernity has been displaced by postmodernity, which inverts many of its core beliefs. An appeal to the intrinsic rationality of faith works well in a modern context, but in other contexts an apologetic approach based on argument and reasoning may well fail to relate with cultural aspirations and prejudices. As we shall see later in this chapter, postmodernity's interest in narrative, rather than argument, offers important possibilities for biblically based apologetics, given the predominance of narrative forms within Scripture.

It remains of vital importance to assert and affirm the reasonableness of faith— without limiting faith to what reason can prove with certainty. The really big questions of life go far beyond what human reason is able to demonstrate. These are questions such as: Who am I? Do I really matter? Why am I here? Can I make a difference?[14] Neither science nor human reason can answer these questions. Yet unless they are answered, life is potentially meaningless. As apologists, we need to show that the Christian faith offers answers to life's big questions, answers that are reasonable on the one hand, and work in practice on the other. There are times when it is just as important to show Christianity is *real* as it is to show it is *true*.

Gateway 3: Stories

A feature of postmodernity that is of particular importance to apologetics is its emphasis on the importance of stories. Modernity was suspicious of the narrative as a means of encountering reality, and sought to repress or displace it through an appeal to rational argument or analysis, shorn of any links with the irritating inconveniences of historical contingency. We can see this with particular clarity in the field of biblical interpretation. As Yale theologian Hans Frei (1922–88) pointed out, the Enlightenment tried to bypass or marginalize the narrative character of Scripture, reducing its historical accounts and narrative forms (such as parables) to essentially timeless ideas.[15] The narrative was seen simply as an irritating and inconvenient shell, obscuring the intellectual and moral kernel of Scripture.

Postmodernity has witnessed a reclamation of interest in the biblical story, including specific narrative forms such as the parables told by Jesus of Nazareth to teach about the kingdom of God. No longer is truth determined by argument; instead, stories are seen as having the capacity to establish a distinctive moral and conceptual identity. Christianity proclaims and inhabits a story-shaped world, with ideas and values grounded in and shaped by the narrative of God's dealings with his people—supremely the narrative of Jesus of Nazareth. Christianity is thus neither simply nor fundamentally a set of ideas.

Since about 1970, there has been increasing interest in exploring the role of narrative in both theology and philosophy. In Anglo-American philosophy, leading writers such as Paul Ricoeur, Alasdair

MacIntyre, and Charles Taylor have taken up the basic themes of narrative with rigor and enthusiasm. Ricoeur has explored the way in which narrative is foundational to any understanding of the world and how humans live in it. MacIntyre argues that our life decisions are shaped and ordered by our sense of how they fit within a larger "story" (or tradition). He famously asserts that "I can only answer the question, 'What am I to do?' if I can answer the prior question, 'Of what story do I find myself a part?' "[16] As we shall see, these approaches can be of enormous value to Christian apologetics.

There is now widespread support for the view that stories are the basic medium through which human beings view reality. Our way of seeing the world is a story that answers fundamental questions of existence, identity, and the future. These stories can give answers to what philosopher Karl Popper calls "ultimate questions." By this, Popper intended us to understand the big "meaning of life" questions, such as those set out by Roy Baumeister.[17] These concern identity, purpose, agency, and value, taking the form of questions such as: "Who am I?" "What is the point of life?" "What can I do to make a difference?"

The cultural and intellectual importance of this idea of a controlling and illuminating narrative has long been recognized. The technical term "myth" is often used in scholarship to refer to such controlling narratives, which offer explanations of reality and conferrals of personal and social identity. (The term "myth" is often misunderstood to mean "an untrue story," which is not what is intended here.) As Lewis and others have pointed out, the word "myth" fundamentally designates a story told about the world that enables individuals to understand and act within that world. These "myths" are the lenses through which a given society looks at the world; they offer a framework upon which the multiple and often contradictory experiences of life may be resolved and correlated.

For Lewis himself, the Christian narrative—which he regarded as the God-given culmination and fulfillment of other human attempts at myth-making—offers the supreme vantage point from which to understand reality. The Christian story of creation, fall, redemption, and consummation makes sense of all other stories we tell about our identity and true goals. It is the master narrative, the supreme story, which positions all other narratives of human origins and destiny.

This point is emphasized by British New Testament scholar and apologist N. T. Wright, who points out that when we tell the whole story of the Bible we are both proclaiming the Christian view of reality and challenging its secular alternatives. By telling the story of the Bible

> we are inevitably challenging more than just one aspect of the world's way of looking at things (i.e., its view of authority and power). We are undermining its entire view of what the world is, and is for, and are offering, in the best way possible, a new world-view.[18]

For Wright, the Bible challenges alternative ways of thinking and commends and embodies its own. It tells a story that answers four fundamental questions:

1. *Who are we?* The Bible tells us we are human beings who are made in the image of our creator, and are not given our fundamental identity by race, gender, social class, or geographical location.
2. *Where are we?* We learn that we live in a good and beautiful, though transient, world, created by the God whose image we bear.
3. *What is wrong?* We discover that humanity has rebelled against its creator, and the world is consequently out of tune with its created intention.
4. *What is the solution?* We are reassured that God has acted, is acting, and will act within creation through Jesus Christ and the Holy Spirit to deal with the evil resulting from human rebellion, and to bring his world to the end for which it was made—namely, that it should resonate fully with his own presence and glory.[19]

A similar view is encountered in the works of novelist J. R. R. Tolkien, noted both for his energetic defense of the necessary role of myth in making sense of reality and his own attempt to apply such thinking in his epic trilogy The Lord of the Rings.[20] In this approach, the explanatory power of the Christian metanarrative is indicated by its ability to position, interpret, and account for other metanarratives. Like all narratives, the Christian story cannot be "proved" by objective rational or scientific means. It has to be judged by its ability to make more sense of things than its present or potential rivals; by its simplicity, elegance, and comprehensiveness; and by its capacity to make sense beyond its own intended focus.

So how does this new interest in narrative help us, as we seek to understand how to express the Christian faith to our culture? Let me offer some personal reflections. When I was younger, I used to believe that the best way to help other people discover the truth and excitement of Christianity was to argue with them—in other words, to persuade them Christianity was right and true. In short, I adopted what many would now call a "modern" approach. But today I would communicate the truth of the gospel in another way. I would tell the story of how I came to faith. Why? Partly because a story is much more interesting than any argument, but more significantly, my story shows that Christianity is *real*—in other words, that it has the capacity to change people's lives, to give them new reasons for living and a firm hope for the future. A story is about a worldview that has been appropriated and that has the power to renew, transform, and excite. By telling my story, I am confirming the gospel is *real* in my life.

***

We live in a world that is shaped by stories. "Grand stories" have the ability to make sense of the world and to position observers and events in a helpful relationship to each other. These stories are nets of meaning we spin, partly to capture and preserve our own experiences, and partly to capture the meaning we believe they convey or signify. Christianity tells one such story and New Atheism tells another; countless other stories are told by those with agendas to pursue, visions to share, or axes to grind. Narratives position realities by locating them within the framework of a story.

Having laid a theoretical foundation for emphasizing the importance of stories to apologetics, we now need to consider how to use them. We will begin shortly by looking at two stories told to bolster the authors' cases against Christianity, and considering how they may be criticized.

Christian apologetics needs to critique other grand stories—such as secular metanarratives that subvert or marginalize Christianity. But it also needs to appreciate how it has stories of its own to tell. The Christian metanarrative of creation, fall, redemption, and consummation helps us make sense of the world—as Lewis and others have demonstrated. But these are "grand narratives." What of *ordinary* stories? How can these sorts of narratives be used in Christian apologetics?

The most obvious place to start is the parables. It is no accident that Jesus of Nazareth used stories to engage with his audiences. These stories were often grounded in the everyday life of the rural farming communities of first-century Palestine. They were immensely accessible stories that engaged the attention and imagination of their audiences. Each of these parables has considerable apologetic potential, which needs to be identified, appreciated, and above all *used*. The parables have the potential to be as powerful today as the day they were first told—if they are used judiciously.

The wise apologist will work through the main parables, asking these critically important questions: How might this story help me communicate the gospel? How might it help me connect with this audience? The issue here is *not* to clarify the parable's imagery and vocabulary in the light of first-century Judaism, but to ask how it can be used apologetically *right now*.

An example will help to make this point clearer. Let's consider the familiar gospel story usually referred to as the "parable of the pearl of great price."

> The kingdom of heaven is like a merchant in search of fine pearls; on finding one pearl of great value, he went and sold all that he had and bought it. (Matt. 13:45–46)

Though sketched with the utmost verbal economy—a mere twenty-five words in the original Greek—the human imagination can easily work on this and appreciate its power. The story rings true to experience and proves easy to develop and apply. So how might we use it apologetically? Let me show you how I would use it, and leave you to work out how you could improve on this:

> We're all looking for something that is really worthwhile in life. Yet often we find that the things we expected to make us happy and

bring us joy do nothing of the sort. So we find ourselves wondering if anything will ever bring us joy and peace. Jesus once told a story about this. A merchant finds a priceless pearl for sale, and decides that he will sell everything in order to possess it. Why? When the merchant saw that special pearl, he knew that everything already in his possession seemed dull and lackluster in comparison. Just as the brilliance of the sun drowns that of the stars, so that they can only be seen at night, so this great pearl allowed the merchant to see what he already owned in a different perspective. What he had thought would satisfy him proved only to disclose his dissatisfaction, and make him long for something that was, for the moment, beyond his grasp. And then he saw that special pearl. He knew he had to have it. He had discovered something of supreme value. Here is finally something worth possessing. Everything else he possesses seems of little value in comparison. Well, that's what the Christian gospel turns out to be like, once you start to explore it. It's something that is so wonderful that it trumps everything else.

Here, a biblical story is used to make an important apologetic point. However, biblical stories can also be used to generate frameworks of meaning or interpretation that can be used to make sense of life. The audience is invited to step inside the story and ask whether it seems to help make sense of their experiences and observations.

But not all biblical stories illuminate single points in this way. Others allow us to see our experience and observations of life in a new way. To illustrate this, let's consider one of the great narratives of the Old Testament: the exile of Jerusalem to Babylon and the final restoration of her people to their homeland after the fall of the Babylonian empire.

One of the most important narratives of the Old Testament concerns the exile of Jerusalem to Babylon in 586 BC. In 605 BC, the Babylonian emperor Nebuchadnezzar defeated the massed Egyptian armies at Carchemish, establishing Babylon as the leading military and political power in the region. Jehoiakim, king of Judah, rebelled against Babylonian rule. Judah was invaded by Babylonian forces, which was clearly interpreted by writers of the time as the execution of the promised judgment of the Lord against his faithless people and king. In early 597 BC, the king, the royal family, and the circle of royal advisors gave themselves up to the besieging forces. They were deported to Babylon along with several thousand other captives. A further wave of deportations took place in 586 BC. Only when Babylon fell to the Persians in 539 BC would the people of Jerusalem be free to return to their homeland.

This powerful historical narrative is often used to make sense of the human situation. From a Christian perspective, the situation of Jerusalem in exile in Babylon is a symbol of the human situation. The people of Jerusalem did not belong in Babylon. They were in exile, longing to return to their homeland. Psalm 137 speaks powerfully of their longing to return and their memories of their native land: "By the rivers of Babylon—there we sat down and there we wept when we remembered Zion" (v. 1).

This framework makes sense of human life. We are not meant to be here. This is not our homeland. We really belong somewhere else. Deep within us, a memory of our homeland persists that nothing is able to eradicate. We have a longing to return to our homeland, and live in the hope that we shall one day be where we really belong. This framework speaks of our true origin and destiny, and makes sense of the deep yearning and longing captured by the "argument from desire."

But what of stories told to challenge Christianity? Let's look at two such stories that have tried to undermine the historical credibility of the traditional Christian account of the significance of Jesus of Nazareth: Dan Brown's *The Da Vinci Code* (2003) and Philip Pullman's *The Good Man Jesus and the Scoundrel Christ* (2010). What are their approaches? And what responses may be offered?

Narratives invite us to imagine alternative worlds and compare them with our own: Which is the more plausible? The more attractive? Such rereadings of history often have polemic or moral motivations, such as a concern to portray a maligned historical figure in a better light, or a beloved figure in a worse one. Robert Graves's novel *I, Claudius* (1934), for example, provided a positive and sympathetic account of the Roman emperor Claudius (10 BC–AD 54), traditionally regarded as a harmless idiot. Graves depicts Claudius as deliberately cultivating this appearance to fool others, thus ensuring his survival and ultimate triumph in a politically dangerous age.

Dan Brown's 2003 blockbuster grabs and holds its readers' attention through a deftly narrated plot, which retells early Christian history with such plausibility that readers are generally unaware of the radical revisions so subtly asserted. (Early printings of the work included the important subtitle *A Novel*. This was later dropped.) Brown's controlling narrative is that of the church inventing and imposing its own view of Jesus as God through political machinations and the threat of violence. The emperor Constantine is portrayed as a Machiavelli, changing the nature of Christianity to meet his own political needs.

Brown spins a story of deceit and suppression, culminating in a denouement that exposes the "truth" and liberates people. Much of the story focuses on the history of early Christianity. According to Brown, the emperor Constantine wanted Christianity to be the official religion of the Roman Empire and realized it needed to be reworked for the purpose. Jesus of Nazareth had to be elevated above the status of a rural peasant teacher. So Constantine declared Jesus was really God. This required fixing votes and fiddling with texts. Readers are introduced to these secrets by Sir Leigh Teabing, who is privy to their history. Nobody ever thought Jesus was divine, Teabing declares, until the Council of Nicaea in 325, when the matter was put to the vote. It only just scraped through. Cryptologist Sophie Neveu is shocked by these words, and says as much: "I don't follow. His divinity?"

> "My dear," Teabing declared, "until *that* moment in history, Jesus was viewed by his followers as a mortal prophet . . . A great and powerful man, but a man nonetheless. A mortal."
>
> "Not the Son of God?" [said Sophie].
>
> "Right," Teabing said. "Jesus' establishment as 'the Son of God' was officially proposed and voted on by the Council of Nicaea."
>
> "Hold on. You're saying Jesus' divinity was the result of a *vote*?"
>
> "A relatively close vote at that," Teabing added.[21]

Teabing explains how Constantine suppressed gospels that spoke of Jesus in purely human terms. Only those that pointed to his divinity were tolerated.[22]

The novel's readers are given access to what they are confidently and confidentially told are suppressed and dangerous facts about the history of the Christian church, focusing on the mysterious Priory of Sion, the guardian of a dark secret. Brown tells his readers it is factually correct that this Priory is a secret society founded in 1099 and still in existence to this day. Wrong on all counts. This organization was invented in 1956 by Pierre Plantard (1920–2000), a fantasist who spun increasingly elaborate stories about his invented community, linking it to earlier events in the Middle Ages and Holy Land.[23] There's nothing factual about it.

I am unaware of any serious historical defense of any of the leading ideas of *The Da Vinci Code*, all of which can be refuted with trivial ease. But that's not the point. Brown tells a story that many would like to be true and invites them to believe it is so. Brown's narrative subverts the traditional Christian account of things at a popular level, portraying it as resulting from the improper exercise of power and a desire to suppress the feminine elements of faith. The real truth about Jesus, we "learn," is that he married Mary Magdalene and their daughter produced a royal bloodline in France. In responding to the many criticisms of rank historical inaccuracy made against the novel, Brown argued that he merely put words into the mouths of his characters and left readers to work out what to make of them.

The appeal of Brown's approach derives mainly from its subversive significance. *The Da Vinci Code* is written in a somewhat clunky style, which most readers seem prepared to tolerate, given the fast-moving plot. The contrast with Philip Pullman's 2010 work *The Good Man Jesus and the Scoundrel Christ* is marked.[24] Pullman's style, modeled partly on that of the King James Bible, possesses an eloquence that is strikingly absent from Brown's clunky, leaden prose.

Pullman's book offers an imaginative retelling of the gospel story, retaining the style of the original Gospels while radically altering their content. This reworking of the gospel narrative involves the introduction of a core hypothesis around which Pullman's thesis is developed. Mary is represented as a simpleton, a girl with learning difficulties tricked into sleeping with a man who assures her he is an angel. She gave birth to twin boys—Jesus and Christ—whose relationship rapidly goes wrong.

Jesus went on to become a saintly man, an itinerant preacher who preached the coming of the kingdom of God and demanded moral transformation from his followers. Like a nineteenth-century liberal Protestant preacher, Pullman tells us that Jesus didn't really perform miracles. He just made things happen naturally. The feeding of the five thousand? They just shared their sandwiches.

Jesus turns out to be a good, otherworldly figure who seems to have little traction on the realities of political power. Christ, however, is different. He encounters a mysterious character—The Stranger—who plants in his mind the idea of rewriting accounts of Jesus's life and teachings to make them more appealing and enduring. The result is a mythical gospel, authored for fundamentally venial reasons by Jesus's imagined twin brother. Pullman's implicit suggestion is that Christ's "improved" and doctored gospel underlies the Pauline literature of the New Testament.

The church is thus founded on the imagined gospel of Christ, not the lost historical realities of Jesus. Christ shrewdly appreciates the need for a metanarrative, a compelling worldview, to sustain the church over the vast timelines of history. Jesus having failed to provide one, Christ supplements this deficiency himself, contriving a story that will securely ground and reinforce an institution. Institutional invulnerability depends upon a divine mandate, ruthlessly enforced and ideologically secured. Pullman's target, as in the His Dark Materials trilogy, is clearly the institutional church.

"The Stranger" eventually prompts Christ to betray his brother to death (and yes, Christ eventually turns out to be Judas Iscariot). The resurrection becomes a piece of theater in which the living Christ tries to pass himself off as the dead Jesus. The resurrection, needless to say, is invented by Christ to compensate for the depressingly ordinary death of Jesus. It's a theme familiar to the readers of rationalist rewritings of the life of Jesus in the eighteenth century, given a new and historically improbable twist by Pullman.

And that's the problem. Pullman's polemical fable is so implausible that it fails even the most trivial criteria of historical authenticity. Pullman's story is so convoluted it cannot be taken seriously as history. When constructing his own narratives, Pullman is a master storyteller. When reworking someone else's story—especially one as familiar as that of Jesus of Nazareth—he struggles. The reconstructed plot is so contrived that even Pullman's considerable stylistic gifts cannot carry off the complex storyline required to sustain his anti-orthodox agenda.

Pullman has clearly inserted himself in the biblical narrative, and he cannot be said to play a passive or silent role. This is perhaps most obvious and intrusive in the reworked prayer of Jesus in Gethsemane, in which Jesus concludes—what a surprise!—that there is no God. Even Pullman's voice becomes tedious and dreary at points such as this, particularly when he preaches vicariously to his readers, using a rather shrill, hectoring tone. It's just not in the same league as His Dark Materials, and seems awfully preachy and predictable at points.

The far-fetched narrative of *The Good Man Jesus and the Scoundrel Christ* is clearly intended to be subversive of institutional religious authority. Pullman's intention is best seen in a question he posed in an interview shortly after the publication of his book: "If you could go back in time and save that man from crucifixion, knowing that that would mean that there would be no church, would you or not?" The argument here rests upon the presumption that the reader shares Pullman's intense dislike for the institutional church, so evident in his earlier publications. But are things *really* that straightforward? And is historical truth really about what we would *like* to be true? And is the gospel *really* about an institutional church?

It is widely known that Pullman wants to undermine the basis of Christian belief. But how does this book advance his argument? The decidedly lukewarm response to this work on atheist websites indicates the ambiguous significance of this work. "But what's the point of it?" one of my atheist academic colleagues asked me recently. "Who's going to take this nonsense seriously?" These are good and obvious questions that frequently flitted through my mind as I enjoyed Pullman's prose while struggling to suspend my disbelief in his cumbersome plotline. I have to confess I have yet to find a persuasive answer.

Gateway 4: Images

For postmodern writers, pictures, rather than words, are the supreme form of communication. Advertising corporations spend fortunes determining the best image for a company. They develop television commercials presenting images that make us want to buy certain products and not others. Many Christians—such as myself—prefer to use words (in my own case, especially the written word) to communicate and commend our faith. Yet we need to be aware that, in our postmodern context, images are seen as having special authority and power, transcending the limitations placed on words.

The human mind works by generating images—images that help us "picture" and make sense of the world around us. Images can be likened to mental maps, helping us to chart the territory of reality and identify our own place on the terrain around us. These images are enormously helpful to the apologist. Intellectual visions of the Christian worldview can often be expressed using images, which have the power to captivate the imagination. We learn to *inhabit* an image, working its angles and finding out how well it fits the realities of our world.

In this section, we shall explore several such images and examine how they can be used to commend and communicate the gospel. Some are drawn from Scripture, some from secular culture. The first such image is taken from a work of classical Greek philosophy— Plato's *Republic*. (If you have read Lewis's Narnia novel *The Silver Chair*, you will already be very familiar with this image, although you may not have realized its historical origins.[25])

Plato asks us to imagine a dark cave, in which a group of people have lived since their birth. They have been trapped there all their lives and know no other world. At one end of the cave, a fire burns brightly, providing them with both warmth and light. As the flames rise, they cast shadows on the walls of the cave. The people watch these shadows projected on the wall in front of them, wondering what they represent. For those living in the cave, this world of flickering shadows is all they know. Their grasp of reality is limited to what they see and experience in this dark prison. If there is a world beyond the cave, it is something they do not know and cannot imagine. Their horizons are limited and determined by the shadows and half-light. Yet they do not know that the cave is a prison, or that they are trapped. Only if they knew of another world could they make such a judgment.

Plato elaborates on this image in a number of ways. The people are chained and restrained so that they cannot move around the cave. They can only see the wall directly ahead of them. Behind them is a walkway, across which people walk, carrying various objects on their heads. The fire casts these moving shadows on the cave walls. The people on the walkway are talking to each other, and the echoes of their voices reverberate around the cave, distorted by its walls. The prisoners thus see moving shadows and hear echoes. They do not see or hear anything *directly*; everything is experienced indirectly and indistinctly.[26]

Yet our interest here is not so much with Plato's philosophical development of this analogy, but with its apologetic potential. How can it be used to commend and communicate the gospel in today's world? Spend a few moments trying to inhabit this image. Remember, you must forget completely about the world we all know—the world of bright sunlight, fresh air, flowers, lakes, and trees. The only world you know is a dark cave. This is what defines reality for you. You see shadows and hear echoes. There is nothing else to see and nothing else to hear. The appearances become the reality.

Make sure you have understood that you do not compare the world of the cave with any other reality—the whole point of the analogy is that you have no knowledge of anything other than the cave. It defines reality for you. When you feel you have gotten used to the image, let's see how it can be explored and applied apologetically.

Ask yourself this question: How could the people in the cave realize that there is another, better world beyond its dark, smoky walls? Think about this for a while, then continue reading when you've worked out some answers.

There are three obvious ways in which the people inside the cave might discover their true situation:

1. Someone comes into the cave from the real world outside to tell its inhabitants about the real world. Apologetically, this corresponds to the idea of divine revelation.
2. The structures of the cave itself contain clues to the existence of a world beyond its walls. Apologetically, this corresponds to arguments for God's existence based on clues in the structure of the world.

3. The prisoners have an intuition that there is a better world than the dark, smoky cave. Apologetically, this corresponds to arguments for God's existence based on human feelings, such as the argument from desire.

In what follows, we shall explore the apologetic potential of each of these, continuing to use the image of the cave as we do so.

First, someone might break into the cave from another world. They would tell us about what that other world is like, using analogies based on the cave. Even better, they might also offer to show us the way out. Or better still, offer to take us out. This approach is characteristic of the Christian doctrine of incarnation, which understands Jesus Christ as the one who enters into the world of human experience and history, both to show us how things really are and to enable us to break free from the world's bonds and limitations. Although this theme is found throughout the New Testament, it is especially significant in John's Gospel, as the following verses indicate:

The Word became flesh and lived among us, and we have seen his glory. (John 1:14)

I am the living bread that came down from heaven. (John 6:51)

The second approach holds that the world of the cave itself is studded with clues and indications that it is not the only world. Like the markings observed by Aristippus on the Rhodian shoreline (p. 122), the walls of the cave might be marked with signs pointing to its origins or true destiny. The cave might show evidence of design or of a complexity that raises fundamental questions about how it came to be there. Its walls might be decorated with designs or other clues to its origins and history.

Third, the observers of the cave themselves may already possess a deeply embedded instinct that there is another world. This might take the form of a deep conviction that there is more to life than the darkness of a smoky cave—or a strong intuition that they were destined for another place. Our desire for something that seems never to be satisfied is one of these hints—a hint that ours is not the only world, and that true fulfillment is not to be found within it.

Our deep sense of a longing that is unquenched by our experiences in this world is a vital clue to our true situation and an invitation to discover the greater reality to which it points.

All three approaches are easily explored and explained using the controlling image of Plato's cave. Each allows the apologist to explore an aspect of the Christian faith and discover how it connects with and makes sense of our experiences of the world, and of our own deepest yearnings and intuitions. This powerful image is easily incorporated into talks, sermons, or lectures, and can be developed in a number of highly creative directions. Other ways of exploring the image can easily be added to the three noted above.

So what other images might be used apologetically? Paul uses a series of powerful images in his letters to help us understand what Christ has done for us through his cross and resurrection. One of these images is that of *adoption*. Paul assures us that, through Christ, we have been adopted as the children of God (Rom. 8:23; Gal. 4:5). This image, drawn from Roman family law, is seen by Paul as casting light on the privileges and place of Christians in their relationship with God.[27] It is an image that demands to be understood in our minds and appreciated in our hearts.

The image of adoption is relatively easy to understand. A family decides to grant a child not born within its bounds the same legal privileges as those children born within its bounds. The adopted children will thus have the same inheritance rights as the natural children. Christians may therefore think of themselves as having been brought within the family of God and granted the same legal privileges as any natural children. And who is the natural child of God? None other than Christ himself. Paul thus makes the powerful point that all God bestowed upon Christ as his Son will eventually be granted to us as children of God:

> We are children of God, and if children, then heirs, heirs of God and joint heirs with Christ—if, in fact, we suffer with him so that we may also be glorified with him. (Rom. 8:16–17)

Therefore, the family marks of God's children are suffering in this life and the promise of glory in the life to come. Glory lies beyond suffering, and we must learn to see suffering as a privilege to be borne gladly as a consequence of our new status as God's heirs.

Yet the image of adoption also appeals to our imaginations and hearts, not just to our minds. It cries out to be imaginatively rendered, not just understood. Adoption is about *being wanted*. It is about *belonging*. These are deeply emotive themes, which resonate with the cares and concerns of many in our increasingly fractured society. To be adopted is to be invited into a loving and caring environment. It is to be welcomed, wanted, and valued. Adoption celebrates the privilege of invitation, in which the outsider is welcomed into the fold of faith and love.

The Pauline image of adoption resonates strongly with the deep human yearning to *belong* somewhere. We need to feel we are accepted and wanted. The importance of this point is frequently emphasized in the writings of Simone Weil. In her work *The Need for Roots*, Weil points to the importance of communities in anchoring personal identity: "To be rooted is perhaps the most important and least recognized need of the human soul."[28] Noted Old Testament scholar Walter Brueggemann takes this thought further when he points out that

> the sense of being lost, displaced and homeless is pervasive in contemporary culture. The yearning to belong somewhere, to have a home, to be in a safe place, is a deep and moving pursuit.[29]

The success of the American television series *Cheers* illustrates this point perfectly. The series, which was based on a bar in Boston, began in 1982 and ran for 271 episodes before ending in 1993. Its immense success centered on the strong sense of community it created.[30] The bar was a place of small talk and smart talk, of refuge and welcome, in which everybody knew you. Outside the bar was a crowd of indistinct, unidentified people. But inside, you were a special person. You mattered to others. You belonged somewhere. The theme song for the series captured this perfectly: you want to be somewhere "where everybody knows your name."

The apologist can thus work the angles of the Pauline image of adoption, pointing to its many levels of meaning. Not only does it illuminate the benefits that the death and resurrection of Christ bring to us; it engages a deep and hugely significant longing of the human heart—to belong somewhere.

Other biblical images could easily be developed apologetically—for example, God as shepherd, or Christ as the bread of life. Apologetics has a rich treasure chest on which to draw, using the imagination as a gateway to the human soul. The good apologist needs to refresh this treasure chest regularly, adding fresh stories and images.

Moving On

The four gateways discussed in this chapter are all important and highly applicable to apologetics. However, these are only illustrative, not exhaustive. Other gateways can easily be added. For example, the way in which Christians live and embody their faith can serve an important apologetic function. Many are moved to ask about faith when they realize that their friends seem to have something they do not—for example, a sense of peace or purpose, or a deep-seated compassion and love for their fellow human beings. "Where did that come from?" they ask, secretly wondering if they could possess it as well. The love of God is both embodied and proclaimed when Christians serve their neighbors or the world.

The way in which Christians approach death is an important witness to the transforming hope of the resurrection, which is of such importance to the Christian gospel. Living out the truth can be thought of as an "incarnational apologetic," itself a powerful witness to that truth. We need more than just arguments; we need to show that the Christian faith is life-changing and life-empowering. As apologist Philip D. Kenneson wisely pointed out:

> What our world is waiting for, and what the church seems reluctant to offer, is not more incessant talk about objective truth, but an embodied witness that clearly demonstrates why anyone should care about any of this in the first place.[31]

Furthermore, Christian living is an important witness to the ability of the gospel to change lives. By being witness to our own story, we are indirectly witnessing that the gospel is *real*, not just something that is *true*.

More approaches could easily be listed. Each apologist can develop them further in the light of the issues he finds himself engaging, or cultural trends to which she feels she must respond. Some obvious examples of further genres with real apologetic potential include:

1. *Films*. Combining both narratives and images, the film is perhaps one of the best means of communicating with a generation whose access to reality is primarily visual rather than textual. Many recent films raise major theological and apologetic issues, offering important openings for apologetic discussions.

2. *Poetry*. Many poems express deep anxieties about the present state of the world and aspirations about the ultimate goal of humanity. It is relatively easy for the apologist to identify poems—including the lyrics of popular songs—that have the potential to raise questions or open apologetic gateways.

3. *Works of art*. Many classical works of art, not to mention popular images, can act as apologetic gateways. For example, a quick internet search will allow you to bring up Edvard Munch's famous painting *The Scream* (1893). It shows a figure in deep existential despair. He—or she?—is unable to cope with the world. What can be done? It's an excellent apologetic gateway. And many others can easily be found.

Having looked at ways in which we can commend the Christian faith and connect it to the lives of ordinary people, we must now consider how to respond to difficulties and anxieties people experience about faith. How should we respond to these?

For Further Reading

Carson, D. A. *The God Who Is There: Finding Your Place in God's Story*. Grand Rapids: Baker, 2010.

Johnston, Robert K. *Reel Spirituality: Theology and Film in Dialogue*, 2nd ed. Grand Rapids: Baker Academic, 2006.

Keller, Timothy J. *The Reason for God: Belief in an Age of Skepticism*. New York: Dutton, 2008.

Marsh, Clive. *Theology Goes to the Movies: An Introduction to Critical Christian Thinking*. New York: Routledge, 2007.

McGrath, Alister E. *Surprised by Meaning: Science, Faith, and How We Make Sense of Things*. Louisville: Westminster John Knox, 2011.

Nash, Ronald H. *Faith and Reason: Searching for a Rational Faith*. Grand Rapids: Academie Books, 1988.

Peters, James R. *The Logic of the Heart: Augustine, Pascal, and the Rationality of Faith*. Grand Rapids: Baker Academic, 2009.

Piper, John. *Think: The Life of the Mind and the Love of God*. Wheaton: Crossway, 2010.

Sire, James W. *Naming the Elephant: Worldview as a Concept*. Downers Grove, IL: InterVarsity, 2004.

Wright, N. T. *Simply Christian: Why Christianity Makes Sense*. San Francisco: HarperSanFrancisco, 2006.

Questions about Faith

DEVELOPING APPROACHES

pologetics is about communicating the joy, coherence, and relevance of the Christian faith on the one hand, and dealing with anxieties, difficulties, and concerns about that faith on the other. This has always been the case, from the time of the New Testament onward.[1] Apologetics insists there are indeed honest and persuasive answers to the honest questions people ask about faith. These questions must be respected and taken seriously. More importantly, they need to be answered. And even more importantly, there are answers that can be given.

The questions and concerns raised about faith vary from one culture to another. Early Christian writers were concerned about how to meet Platonist criticisms of their beliefs on the one hand, and how to develop effective ways of communicating and commending their faith to Platonists on the other. Many western European theologians of the early Middle Ages—including the great Thomas Aquinas—focused on apologetic questions raised by Muslim writers. (At that time, Islam was a significant presence in Spain and southern France.) Once more, we have to appreciate the importance of the audience for apologetics. The nature of the audience shapes the questions that might be asked about Christianity, just as it will shape the way in which the Christian faith is presented.

In an Islamic context, for example, questions are often raised about the history of the church (especially around the time of the Crusades), the doctrine of the Trinity, and the divinity of Christ. These two latter doctrinal points are widely seen to be in conflict with core Islamic teachings about the unity of God.

In a rationalist context, questions are often raised about beliefs that seem to be "irrational" (such as the doctrine of the Trinity or the characteristic Christian belief that Jesus is both divine and human), or that seem to call the fundamental goodness or autonomy of human nature into question (such as the doctrine of original sin). In a postmodern context, questions are likely to be raised about the New Testament's emphasis on Jesus Christ being the only way to salvation (which is held to be inconsistent with postmodernism's positive appraisal of diversity).

The important point is to understand your audience, and appreciate its concerns and questions. You should not see these as unwelcome *threats*, but rather welcome them as possible gateways to faith. When someone asks you a question, it's important to see this as a signal of interest and a willingness to listen. Perhaps your questioner hopes to demolish you with a lethal challenge; nevertheless, you are being given an opening for the gospel, which it is crucial to value and engage. These questions give you the opportunity to open up some of the great riddles of life, and in doing so, begin to explain and commend the Christian vision of reality. There is no need to adopt a defensive attitude when defending Christianity. Rather, see each question as an opportunity to remove misunderstandings, explain the reliability and appeal of faith, and talk about its impact on life. Questions must be welcomed and good answers developed and given. They're already there. We need only to discover them, and adapt them to our own gifts as speakers and to the specific audiences we're engaging.

So how are we to engage these questions? Some apologetics textbooks offer standard answers to equally standard questions, encouraging readers to master these routine responses in order to become faithful and effective defenders of the Christian faith.[2] As a professional educationalist, I have to confess I prefer a different approach. The best responses to the questions people ask us about our faith are not those borrowed from textbooks or based on industry-standard templates, but are those developed by individual apologists as they reflect on the questions being asked, the situations of the people asking them, and the resources available to answer them. Apologists cannot be content to depend on borrowed answers. They need to develop answers for themselves. In short, they need to *own* their answers. Never give an answer to a question that doesn't satisfy you in the first place.

This chapter does not provide a detailed list of difficulties about faith and answers you might give. It sets out to encourage you to develop your own answers. It aims to teach you a *method*, not provide you with a prepackaged set of answers to cut and paste into your apologist's mind. We shall first look at some general principles about engaging with questions, anxieties, and concerns.

But before we begin considering such questions, we need a framework we can use to make sense of our own role as apologists. A visual image will help us think about this. Many apologists find they get discouraged when they give what they believe to be good answers to honest questions—yet seem to have no obvious impact on their audience. Surely if a good answer is given, there is nothing to stop that person from coming to faith immediately? Sadly, life turns out to be rather more complicated than this simple model suggests.

An image I have long found helpful is to think of each person potentially being on a road leading from doubt or unbelief to faith. For some, that path is smooth and easy, having few roadblocks of any importance. For others, that path is long and difficult, with many potholes and other obstacles to faith along the way. The problem is that an external observer doesn't know what someone's road looks like; the apologist has no idea whether the difficulty raised by the person she's speaking to is the one and only remaining barrier to faith—or whether a whole series of difficulties remain to be engaged. All the apologist can do is give a good answer and trust that a seed has been sown—and that one less barrier to faith remains. Our job is to move people along by one step. For some, this is the final step; for others, it is merely one step further along their road. But they are now nearer than they were! The apologist's job is thus to walk with someone along that road to faith, leaving him or her closer to its goal than when they started.

Later in this chapter, we will look at two specific case studies of objections and anxieties about Christianity that are often raised in discussion. These have been chosen to be representative of genuine concerns, while at the same time allowing us to reflect on how good answers can be developed.

Questions and Concerns: Some Basic Points

In dealing with questions, it is helpful to set them in perspective and realize how best to deal with them. Most apologists find they become much better at recognizing and responding to questions with experience.

1. Be gracious.

Paul reminds us we are "ambassadors for Christ" (2 Cor. 5:20). We need to remember we should model the values of the gospel in our response to people. God's graciousness needs to be on display here, not human arrogance or impatience! Try to give polite, considerate, and helpful replies, especially if the question suggests that the person asking it doesn't really understand the Christian faith, or has an inflated view of his own intellectual prowess.

2. What is the real question?

Apologists are often told to try and work out the question behind the question. What does that mean? Let's imagine you've been asked a question about how a good God can allow suffering in the world. The questioner may see this as a genuine intellectual difficulty and want a good philosophical answer. Make sure you can give one!

But this might not be the case. The questioner could have sat at her mother's bedside for night after night watching her suffer great pain in the final stages of bone cancer before dying—last week. Her perspective is not intellectual curiosity, but deep personal anguish. She isn't going to want a philosophy lecture from you! She's going to want sympathy and understanding. The answer she is looking for may well need to be existential rather than intellectual—in other words, reassuring her of God's presence in the shadowlands of life.

One way of dealing with this issue that I have found helpful is to welcome the question, and then ask the questioner if he would mind sharing why this is a particular concern for him. This helps me work out what the real question is and address it properly.

3. Don't give prepackaged answers to honest questions.

It's tempting to learn responses to a list of questions by rote, and use these when responding to people's questions about faith. But this is not effective, for two very good reasons. First, you'll end up sounding like some kind of preprogrammed machine, churning out routine answers that are not adapted to the specific audience. And second, your stock answer may not fit the question being asked. You are heard to answer a different question. Audiences notice this kind of thing and find it unsatisfactory and unpersuasive. We apologists need to *listen*, and make sure we really engage with the question being asked, which may force us to adapt and develop our "standard" answer.

4. Appreciate the importance of learning from other apologists.

One of the most worthwhile things I do with my students at the Oxford Center for Christian Apologetics is to get a group of between six and twelve of them together to discuss what we might say to a series of questions people ask us. I'll pose a question in advance, and the students take a few minutes to draft their replies. We then work through all the responses, looking at both their style and substance. The result? Not only does this give students experience responding to questions; more importantly, they are exposed to a dozen or so different ways of engaging an important question. Everyone goes away with a better understanding of how we can respond helpfully to such concerns.

One of the best ways of developing your responses to concerns and objections to faith is to learn from others who have developed the art of apologetics—such as William Lane Craig, Peter Kreeft, or Ravi Zacharias. You can easily find video or audio recordings of their lectures, including responses to questions, on the internet.

Listen to their responses to questions from the audience. Note both the *tone* and the *content* of their responses. It's not just what you say that matters; it's how you say it.

To help you develop your own method, we are going to explore some questions that arise naturally in apologetic presentations and conversations, and some possible approaches. This analysis is neither comprehensive nor profound. It just helps you to get an idea of some possible approaches to each question, and work out what you yourself would say. In each case we will identify some of the basic building blocks you might incorporate into your response. These are the threads; how you weave them together will reflect both your own approach to apologetics and the specific questions you need to engage. We begin by considering the problem of suffering.

Case Study 1: Why Does God Allow Suffering?

Our first case study is an issue that is regularly raised both in public debates and private conversations. If God is good, why is there suffering in the world? Why do bad things happen in a universe created by a supposedly loving God? It's an important question in its own right. Yet it also allows us to reflect on how we go about framing answers to all of the questions we get asked.

In what follows, we'll look at a portfolio of points that can be made in response to the question of suffering. Each is a thread that can be used on its own or woven with others as part of the pattern of a richer tapestry.

Let's begin by asking why so many people find the existence of suffering to be a problem. At first sight, this seems very straightforward. There seems to be a logical contradiction here. If God is good, why is there evil in the world? For some, this is the real issue that needs to be addressed. Is faith vulnerable at this point? This question needs a reasoned, logical response.

But as we noted earlier, the existence of suffering raises anxieties for some people at a much deeper level. They are confused and distressed by the suffering or death of someone they love. Logic doesn't really interest them that much. The problem is not so much understanding suffering as *coping* with it. Their anxiety is not so much that the Christian faith might be illogical, as that the universe might be meaningless. As comedian Woody Allen once wryly remarked: "More than any other time in history, mankind faces a crossroads. One path leads to despair and utter hopelessness. The other, to total extinction. Let us pray we have the wisdom to choose correctly."

The apologist needs to be aware that this question has to be addressed at different levels. A cold, clinical dissection of the intellectual issues may be helpful to some people; it will leave others bewildered and confused, precisely because their concern is *existential* rather than *intellectual*. For many people, the experience of suffering is a problem of the heart rather than a problem of the mind. The question they are concerned with is not "How do I make sense of this intellectually?" but "How do I cope with this existentially?"[3] Emotional empathy as much as intellectual wisdom is clearly needed here!

The first point that needs to be made is that we often have to learn to live with questions. Nobody has a knockdown answer to the problem of suffering. For militant atheist Richard Dawkins, suffering is pointless and meaningless—and is exactly what we should expect in a universe that itself has no purpose. We just need to get used to this. It's a tidy answer, but it leaves many deeply dissatisfied. We just have to learn to rise above the pain and meaninglessness of the world. For many Stoic writers of the ancient world, human beings had to invent their own personal worlds of meaning in the midst of a pointless and absurd world. And that was the best we could hope to do—superimpose meaning on an essentially random and purposeless world.

Some atheists argue that the existence of suffering is evil and therefore is in itself adequate to disprove the existence of God. This is a curious argument, since closer examination shows that it is self-defeating. An argument from the existence of evil to the nonexistence of God depends on establishing that suffering is indeed evil. But this is not an empirical observation—it is a moral judgment. Suffering is natural; for it to be evil, a moral framework has to be presupposed. But where does this framework come from? The argument requires the existence of an absolute moral framework if it is to work. Yet the existence of such an absolute framework is itself widely seen as pointing to God's existence. In the end, the nonexistence of God seems to end up depending on God's existence. It's not the best argument. Yet if it's simply my personal perception that nature is evil, this has no relevance to the debate about God. It might simply say something about my naïve and sentimental tastes rather than about the deeper structure of the universe.

We need to go deeper here. Christianity declares that God suffered in Christ. In other words, God knows what it is like to suffer. The letter to the Hebrews talks about Jesus being someone who suffers along with us (Heb. 4:15). While this does not explain suffering, it certainly makes it more tolerable to bear. It expresses the deep insight that God suffered firsthand as we suffer. In the incarnation, God the creator enters into this world of pain and suffering—not as a curious tourist, but as a committed Savior. Christians thus recognize that God's loving commitment to a suffering world was so great that God entered into it personally—not sending some representative, but choosing to share in its pain and suffering. Famous novelist and amateur theologian Dorothy L. Sayers made this point well when she commented:

> For whatever reason God chose to make man as he is—limited and suffering and subject to sorrows and death—He had the honesty and the courage to take His own medicine. Whatever game He is playing with His creation, He has kept his own rules and played fair. He can exact nothing from man that He has not exacted from Himself. He has Himself gone through the whole of human experience, from the trivial irritations of family life and the cramping restrictions of hard work and lack of money to the worst horrors of pain and humiliation, defeat, despair and death.[4]

God *chose* to suffer. The suffering of Jesus Christ can reassure us that we have the privilege of relating to a God who knows the pain and sorrow of living in a fallen world. The passion stories of the Gospels tell of a Savior who really understands suffering and who has been through it himself. And the psalms speak of a God who is with us always as we journey, even through the darkest moments (Ps. 23).

There is a famous saying about the medical profession: "Only the wounded physician can heal." Whether this is true or not is, of course, a matter for debate. But it does highlight the fact that we are able to relate better to someone who has shared our problem, who has been through what we are going through now—and triumphed over it. As many already know from experience, it is often difficult to relate to someone who hasn't shared our problem. One way of dealing with this apologetically is through empathy. You *empathize* with the other person's problems and fears. Even though you haven't shared them—and may not even be able to understand them!—you try to think yourself into their situation, so you can truthfully tell them you understand exactly how they must be feeling. Yet the central Christian idea of the incarnation speaks of God *sympathizing* with our sufferings—not empathizing, as if God hadn't experienced them firsthand. God sympathizes, in the strict sense of "suffers alongside," with us. In turning to God, we turn to one who knows and understands.

There is a splendid story often told about East Anglia, which was once the center of England's wool trade. During the later Middle Ages, a dead shepherd would be buried in a coffin stuffed full of wool from his own sheep. Why? So that, when the day of judgment came, Christ would see the wool and realize this man had been a shepherd. As Christ himself had once been a shepherd, he would know the pressures the man had faced, the amount of time needed to look after wayward sheep, and would understand why he hadn't been to church very much! Amusing though the story is, it does, however, make an important point, which we must treasure as one of the most precious of the many Christian insights into God: we are not dealing with a distant God who knows nothing of what being human, frail, and mortal means. God knows and understands, so we can "approach the throne of grace with boldness" (Heb. 4:16).

Furthermore, the Christian gospel declares with passion and power that the suffering and pain of this world will give way to a better place—a place in which God "will wipe every tear" from our eyes. "Death will be no more; mourning and crying and pain will be no more" (Rev. 21:4). We live in hope.

These reflections help to set suffering in context. We can also address some aspects of suffering quite persuasively. For example, it is important to make the point that we live in a fallen world in which humans no longer live as God intended them to. Human selfishness and greed have led to wars, famine, overexploitation of the land,

and fundamental and potentially damaging changes to the world's resources. None of these are things God wished to happen. They are things human beings have done. It is often pointed out we have developed a technology that could allow us to make ourselves extinct. That's our choice, not something God wanted.

Furthermore, it is also important to appreciate that suffering arises from the way this world is. We have no reason to believe there could be a "better" world. For example, scientists believe that for life to exist on earth, we need "tectonic plates"—in other words, the earth's surface needs to be able to shift in response to geological pressures. The result? Earthquakes and tsunamis. Are these *evil*? No, they're just *natural*. They can cause suffering. But they're not intended to. It's part of the price we pay for living in a world in which life is possible. Some critics of God mutter darkly about God's failure to create a world that meets their design specifications. If they were in charge, things would be much better! Yet these earnest people seem to be blind to the inconvenient fact that there is absolutely no reason to suppose that a better world could be created, or that a better world exists anywhere else!

Yet there is a much deeper point here. *Why* do we feel disturbed by the suffering of others? *Why* do we feel there is something so *wrong* about suffering? This is a matter of the heart, rather than the head. Where does this deep-seated intuition that suffering and pain are not right come from? As we saw in our reflections about the argument from desire and argument from morality, profound intuitions such as this one are much more significant than many admit. If they are random and meaningless, our perception about the world has no inherent value.

But what if this intuition points to something deeper—something built into us that reflects our true nature and identity? What if it is an aspect of the "homing instinct for God" we noted earlier? What if this revulsion against suffering and pain is a reminder of paradise on one hand, and an anticipation of the New Jerusalem on the other? What if our thoughts about the present state of things are shaped by our intuitive realization of our true origins and destiny?

The issue of suffering thus opens up some very important apologetic questions, as well as some significant opportunities. Yet ultimately, this is a question that *nobody*—whether secular or religious—can answer totally. The real issue concerns who can offer the most existentially satisfying answer, which stands up to critical reflection despite leaving some questions unanswered—perhaps because, given our human limitations, they are ultimately unanswerable. A willingness to live with unresolvable questions is a mark of intellectual maturity, not a matter of logical nonsense as some unwisely regard it.

Later in this chapter, we'll reflect on how to work the angles of this question. How can these ideas be used apologetically? But first, we'll move on to sketch the issues relating to another classic question of apologetics: Is belief in God just a crutch to help inadequate people get through life?

Case Study 2: God as a Crutch

One of the most familiar criticisms of Christianity is that it offers consolation to life's losers. The only way such sad people can cope with life, it is argued, is by inventing a God who comforts them. Real people don't need such spurious reassurance. They just get on with life. Religion is for the emotionally inadequate—a crutch for those who can't cope with the reality of life and prefer to invent their own imagined world.

It is important to note that this criticism is actually an *assertion*, rather than a carefully reasoned or evidence-based argument. There is no scientific proof for any such claim. Nevertheless, it has cultural plausibility for many and is frequently encountered in debates and arguments. So how are we to respond to it?

First, we need to understand its historical origins. Where does this criticism come from? As might be expected, its modern statements are found in the writings of atheist psychoanalyst Sigmund Freud (1856–1939). For Freud, belief in God is an illusion. Freud argues that God exists only in the human mind. The idea of God is a "wish fulfillment," resulting from our desire for meaning and love.

> We tell ourselves that it would be very nice if there were a God who created the world and was a benevolent Providence, and if there were a moral order in the universe and an after-life; but it is the very striking fact that all this is exactly as we are bound to wish it to be.[5]

In other words, we invent a make-believe world that corresponds to our desires, instead of reconciling ourselves to the harshness of the real world around us.

In popular writings, this is often expressed in terms of God being a delusion (as per Richard Dawkins) or a crutch. This second approach has significant rhetorical force, as it implies that those who believe in God are inadequate, wounded people who need help to cope with the realities of life—and who invent God as a spurious psychological means of support. Freud declares (though without any obvious empirical evidence) that our concept of—and attitudes toward—God are infantile illusions, shaped by our experiences of our own fathers. Immature people never grow out of their childish trust in and dependence upon their father and naturally transfer this dependency to an imaginary "enormously exalted father." Freud makes it clear that he regards such a belief in God as intellectually naïve:

> The whole thing is so patently infantile, so foreign to reality, that to anyone with a friendly attitude to humanity it is painful to think that the great majority of mortals will never be able to rise above this view of life.[6]

We find much the same contemptuous attitude in New Atheism, particularly in Richard Dawkins's *The God Delusion* (2006). Yet when all is said and done, this is simply an *assertion*—an assertion that derives its cultural credibility not from empirical evidence, but from the frequency with which it is repeated on one hand, and the confidence with which it is asserted on the other.

Evidential basis for this bold assertion that God is merely the projection of a childish wish for the protection of a father is practically zero. Freud's scientific credentials have been severely criticized in recent years, as it has become increasingly clear that his "scientific investigations" often amounted to little more than retrospective validation of his prejudices, especially his hostility toward belief in God. Freud sets out from the assumption that there is no God, and then seeks to show that a rational explanation may be found for why people do believe in such a nonexistent God. Yet there is an obvious confusion here about whether atheism is the presupposition or the conclusion of this decidedly unsatisfactory piece of reasoning.

But obvious and embarrassing lack of evidential foundations aside, how valid are these arguments? How coherent is Freud's position? There seems to be an obvious problem with Freud's theory— specifically, in his curious idea of a universal, subconscious Oedipal desire within males to kill their father and marry their mother. On the basis of this aspect of his thinking, males would seem to have at least as plausible a psychological basis for wanting to do away with any "father in heaven" as wanting to believe in him. According to Freud, people have both positive and negative feelings toward this "exalted father," and these negative feelings might cause the wish that God not exist to be as strong as the wish for his existence.

Where Freud regarded religious belief as an illusion, C. S. Lewis regarded Freud's atheistic materialism as self-refuting. After all, this argument about "projection" or "invention" cuts both ways. Freud argues that God is a wish fulfillment, in which a heavenly father takes care of all our needs. Yet it is just as logical and evidence-based to argue that Freud and other atheists deny the existence of God out of a need to escape from a father figure they don't like. After all, Freud's relationship with his own father was somewhat strained. It is not difficult to argue that belief in the nonexistence of God springs from his deep desire that no father figure exists. Or that, if such a figure exists, he can be—and ought to be—murdered, perhaps?

Furthermore, Freud fails to do justice to the complexity of human ambivalence about God. After all, the truth that God is loving is a disclosure of revelation, not a natural human insight. As Martin Luther and John Calvin both insist, the more natural human instinct is to be *fearful* of God. Lewis argues that Freud fails to recognize there is a psychological dynamic of fear fulfillment as much as wish fulfillment.[7] People have reasons to wish God *not* exist as well as to wish for his existence. Thus, when he was an atheist, Lewis was quite clear that he regarded God as someone he did *not* want to meet: "Amiable agnostics will talk cheerfully about 'man's search for God.' To me, as I then was, they might as well have talked about the mouse's search for the cat."[8]

Much more seriously, Freud's "argument" amounts to little more than an assertion that human belief in God is consistent with atheism.

But it is also consistent with other systems of thought—most notably, with the Christian belief that God created us with a homing instinct for heaven. To quote from the prayer of Augustine of Hippo, which we noted earlier: "You have made us for yourself, and our heart is restless until it finds its rest in you." Freud argues that atheism can account for belief in God, or a human yearning for God. Perhaps it can, although it all seems a little forced and contrived at points. Yet Christianity accounts for this belief and yearning in a far more coherent and plausible way.

But let's end by focusing on the image of the crutch. It's a rhetorical device, and its message is simple: God is for the emotionally and intellectually crippled. Strong and healthy people don't need this sort of bogus support or specious comfort. They're able to look after themselves. God is just for the weak and foolish. It's pretty much the same message we find in New Atheism, which prides itself on the intellectual excellence of its leading gurus, such as Richard Dawkins and Christopher Hitchens.

Two important points need to be made here. First, the issue is that of *truth*, not *need*. Christian apologists have always insisted that the claims of Christianity are firmly grounded in the bedrock of truth. Historically, relationally, existentially, and intellectually, the Christian faith tells things the way they really are. Part of that total vision of reality includes the important idea that human beings are made in the "image of God," and thus possess an inbuilt tendency to find our way back to God—whether we like it or not.

Second, if you have a broken leg, you *need* a crutch. If you're ill, you *need* medicine. That's just the way things are. The Christian understanding of human nature is that we are damaged, wounded, and disabled by sin. That's just the way things are. Augustine of Hippo compared the church to a hospital. It was, he suggested, full of wounded and ill people who were being healed. Freud seems to argue that he and other atheists are simply better human beings who lack any need for support. But this is just smug nonsense that runs away from reality. It denies the darker side of human beings, to which contemporary culture bears disturbing witness. People are addicted to sex, power, and narcotics—to mention only three categories of things that cause us to forfeit our independence and become their servants.

Whether Freud likes it or not, there is something terribly *wrong* with human nature. It needs its wounds to be bandaged, its sores to be washed, its diseases to be healed, and its guilt to be purged. The image of the crutch summarizes our need for intervention, which is grounded in the realization that we need help—even if we are too proud and complacent to ask for it. Freud wrote much of his more naïve material about human nature after the end of the First World War, in 1918, and before the dawn of the Nazi era in Germany and Austria in the 1930s. Many would argue that the rise of Hitler would have caused Freud to review some of his more idealistic ideas about human nature. Freud died long before anyone knew about Auschwitz and the Nazi death camps.

Yet Freud himself appears to have been aware of a problem here. Even as early as 1913, Freud expressed concern that psychoanalysts were not "themselves better, nobler, or of stronger character."[9] We see here a tacit admission that Freud's remedy for the human problem does not appear to have worked for those best qualified to practice it. A question of "physician, heal thyself," perhaps?

Working the Angles: Applying the Case Studies

In the previous two sections of this chapter we have explored some themes relating to two classic questions of Christian apologetics and identified some components of answers to two important anxieties about faith. But apologetics is as much an art as it is a science. It's not just about knowing arguments; it's about how you use them. There's a helpful analogy here with a medical practitioner: she will have a deep knowledge of the theory of medicine, including both what can go wrong with the human body and what can be done to sort things out. But this science of medicine has limited use unless you can get your patient to tell you what the problem really is.

As many of my medical colleagues complain, their patients often seem reluctant to tell them what their real problems are. Perhaps people are embarrassed by their symptoms, or maybe they are afraid of the possible implications of those symptoms. Every experienced medical practitioner knows the importance of cultivating the art of a good bedside manner: being a good and attentive listener, gaining patients' confidence, and enabling them to disclose their anxieties. They have to find out what the real problems are. It's an art that has to be learned the hard way—by experience.

Apologetics is like that. Knowing apologetic arguments, ideas, and approaches is only part of the task of the effective apologist. The best apologists are those who marry a rigorous knowledge of the science of apologetics with a deep appreciation of the art of apologetics. And here's the difficult bit: you can learn the ideas from books and lectures, but you can only learn the art by practice, by trial and error—in short, by *doing* apologetics. Apologetics is like baking cakes, laying bricks, and playing the piano: you learn them by doing them. In each case, there is a theoretical element. Yet the theory leads into and informs the practice.

It is both impossible and irresponsible for someone such as myself to provide model answers to questions and objections. Not only does this reduce apologetics to learning a few replies by rote, it also fails to realize that each question is different and demands to be taken seriously *on its own terms*. We must listen carefully before we reply. For example, consider the following questions and anxieties, all of which relate directly to the issue of suffering—yet come from different places and need their own distinct responses. Read these questions. Try to work out where the questioner is coming from.

1. "I don't see how a good God can allow suffering. It just doesn't make sense. Can you explain why?"
2. "My mother died last week after a long illness. I prayed to God a lot during her illness. I find it so difficult to believe in a loving God in that kind of situation. Can you help me?"
3. "I read C. S. Lewis's *The Problem of Pain* when I was younger, and really benefited from it. Yet my wife became seriously ill recently. I was devastated. It just seemed to me that Lewis's answer was too slick. It was too neat. It just didn't help me when my world was thrown into turmoil by events. Where do I go from here?"
4. "The Bible tells us that God loves us. But I sometimes find it hard to see that. Why is there all this pain? Why are there earthquakes? Surely a loving God would protect us from this sort of stuff, right?"

Study each of these questions carefully. First, notice that there is little in any of the questions to indicate whether the person asking it is a Christian, an agnostic, or an atheist. This is a very common apologetic dilemma. The question doesn't necessarily tell you whether it's coming from a believer with doubts and questions—or from an atheist who's out to discredit you. You have to make a judgment about how you respond.

Second, note how a stock reply won't meet the very different issues raised by these questions. Each has to be taken on its own terms. You need to work out what might lie behind them. Let's take the third question, for example, which raises an issue of real importance about the approach C. S. Lewis adopts in *The Problem of Pain*, which speaks of suffering as God's "megaphone to rouse a deaf world."[10] Lewis's point is good. Yet many feel that this approach is a little simplistic and inadequate when confronted with the brutal, harsh reality of suffering—including, of course, Lewis himself, after the death of his wife from cancer. His famous work *A Grief Observed* is a powerful critique of his own earlier approach. Yet Lewis did not lose his faith; if anything, it matured and grew through his tragedy. In responding to this question, you could talk about Lewis's changing (and increasingly realistic and engaged) attitude toward suffering, and how he accommodated it within his faith.

The *art* of apologetics extends the reach of the *science* of apologetics. It helps us to make connections with people. When dealing with any concern about faith—such as the two we have just been looking at—we must avoid offering a stock answer and try to tailor our reply to the specific question we have been asked.

1. Try to understand why this question represents a *problem* for someone. Is it because he hasn't understood what Christianity teaches at this point? Is it because her history makes this a particularly significant concern—for example, the issue of suffering might be especially important for someone whose best friend died recently. And try to work out whether this is the real question or whether there's something else beneath the surface.

2. Now work the angles of the question. Try to work out which of the response points noted in our case studies might be particularly important.

3. Now try to set this out in a way adapted to this specific audience. Think of what illustrations you might use, what authors you might quote, and what life experiences might help frame your answer.

4. Now work out what you are going to say.

The fourth step is the hard part. For a start, there is so much we want to say. How can we pack all our ideas into a single answer? When I started out as an apologist, I found it very helpful to begin by writing out in full a response to a question I had found to be important. I would then read it aloud and try to tidy it up so it sounded better. Remember, written and spoken English are very different! Suppose this response took nine minutes to give. I would then try to reduce it to four minutes, aiming to keep the best bits, and make it as punchy and relevant as possible. Finally, I'd try to reduce it to two minutes.

Why? Partly because this forced me to focus on what needed to be said, rather than what I would like to say. But mostly because people find long answers wearying, and much prefer succinct, engaging replies to encyclopedic lectures. When you see the eyes of your audience glazing over with boredom, you know you're in trouble.

Yet for many, the problem is not the length of time it takes to give a good answer, but how you work out the good answer in the first place. When I answer questions after a talk, I often find I have to think on my feet and respond very quickly. Yet twenty-five years of experience of doing this has really helped. I've had to wrestle with most questions, and have worked out what I can say helpfully. The main challenge is to make sure I connect with the question being asked in a helpful and gracious manner. It's an art I've had to learn by doing.

In what follows, we shall explore two genuine questions and the response I gave to each. The replies are relatively short—about two or three minutes long. Then I will explain why I chose to respond in this specific way. I suggest that you read each question and work out what you would say. Then read what I said, and try to reverse engineer my response. Why do you think I gave that answer? Why did I choose those particular colors from the apologetic palette? Then move on, and read my own comments about both question and response. In both cases, these are questions from an audience after a talk I gave in Oxford in 2007 responding to Richard Dawkins's book *The God Delusion* (2006).

Question One

"I have a real problem with God and the suffering of the world. It's so hard to make sense of things. I don't think he really cares about us! Why can't he just take suffering away from us?"

My Answer

"Thank you for that question. I'm sure that there are others in the audience with very similar thoughts and concerns. Let me try and say some things that might be helpful here. First, we *all* have a problem with suffering. It seems wrong and out of place. We have this deep feeling that it's not the way things are meant to be. But part of the Christian hope is that we will one day be in a place where there is no suffering or pain. All these things will have gone. That's where we really belong. This world is like a dark valley of sorrow. Yet Christians know that at the far end of this lies the New Jerusalem, a place of peace. That hope keeps us going as we travel through what the Bible calls the 'valley of the shadow of death.'

"And there's a second point: God does care for us. He is with us as we travel. As a Christian, I believe passionately that we see God in Jesus Christ. God entered into this world of pain, sorrow, and death. That's what the idea of the incarnation is all about. And that means that God chose to come where we are. He chose to share our pain and sorrow. He doesn't send some sidekick to tell us he cares for us. He journeys to where we are, and tells us in person. Jesus suffered on the cross so that one day we can be in a place in which suffering is no more. Now there's much more I need to say about this. But the really important thing is that God leads us through suffering into glory. And he's with us as we travel. We aren't on our own."

Question Two

"You said that God wasn't a delusion. But anyone who knows anything about psychology will tell you that we invent things to suit our need. We make up ideas, and God is no exception. Why don't we just recognize this and face up to things?"

My Reply

"That's a very interesting question, and it opens up lots of important issues. Let me just focus on a few things and make sure that I address the central point you raised. I'm not sure I would agree with your summary of modern psychology, but I agree that we are often tempted to invent ideas that we find consoling. When I was an atheist myself—some years ago now—I took the view that God was just a comforting idea invented by sad people who couldn't cope with the harshness of life. In fact, I took some pleasure in pointing out the metaphysical austerity of atheism. After all, I argued, this was such a bleak outlook on life that nobody would want to invent it!

"Let me just say two things in response to this excellent question. First, I have colleagues who are atheists precisely because they don't want God to exist. They want to construct their own worlds, and decide what's right and what's wrong. God would just get in the way, and make things complicated for them. They know what they *want* to be true; so they declare that it *is* true. So I think this argument cuts both ways. *If* it's right—and that's an open question, by the way—it explains why atheists don't believe in God and theists do believe in God.

"And second, we need to check things out against the evidence. I didn't become a Christian because I felt any need for God. If anything, I was like someone who believed there was only stagnant pond water to drink, who then discovered champagne! What moved me to faith was reflection on the world, not some kind of existential inadequacy on my part. I was perfectly happy to accept a bleak outlook on life—if this was clearly *right*. In the end, I came to faith in God because I believed that this was right. Now I know that sounds like a very intellectual kind of conversion. I had yet to discover that Christianity had imaginative and emotional depth, as well as a capacity to make sense of things. That came later. But that's another story.

"So I certainly agree with you that we need to face up to reality and check things out. You and I are clearly both critical thinkers. I think the big difference between us is where we believe that process of critical thinking takes us!"

———————

Let me make it clear that these are not model answers, applicable to just about every situation. They are real answers, forged in the heat of the moment, which seemed appropriate to those specific questions in the form in which they were raised. Why did I choose to answer the questions in that way? From our engagement with these two concerns, it is clear there are lots of points I could have made. So why did I limit myself to those particular colors on my palette? One obvious reason is that answers to questions need to be fairly short. This limits the number of points you can make. I just couldn't pack all the points I noted earlier in this chapter into those short replies.

Let's look at the first response. As I listened to the person asking this question, I felt that the problem was existential rather than intellectual. The words suggested there was an intellectual component to the question; his demeanor suggested the problem lay deeper. I felt he was not really asking about the possible irrationality of belief in God, but the possible meaninglessness of the universe—and of his own life. In my response, I therefore highlighted the core theme of the presence of God in times of darkness, doubt, and loneliness, before going on to emphasize the key role of the doctrine of the incarnation in affirming God's commitment to us. I ended by emphasizing a single point: "We aren't alone," because that is what I felt this person needed to hear.

Notice I didn't defend God in the face of suffering. I felt the appropriate thing was to show this person how the Christian faith faces up to suffering and has important things to say. As an apologist, I have often found that explaining what Christianity has to say on any given matter is one of its most effective defenses.

What about the second response? As I listened to my questioner, it seemed clear to me he placed great value on reason and evidence, and was inclined to think that belief in God was poorly supported by either. The implicit assumption behind his question was that my faith in God was a delusion. I chose to respond initially by making the point that we often collude with our desires and create reality according to our taste. As I made clear, my questioner needed to consider the possibility that people who *don't* believe in God are simply transmuting their desires into a worldview.

I then told a story—my own story, although only briefly and partially. The main point I wanted to make was that my conversion, at least in my own view, was a movement *toward* reason and evidence, not *away* from them. I also wanted to sow a seed—namely, the suggestion that atheism is actually a rather bleak perspective on life, and that some are unwise enough to assume that the harshness and austerity of a way of looking at things are indicators of its truth. They're not!

Those are my "live" answers—developed then and there, in response to genuine questions from an audience. I hope they were helpful. But I am sure you will believe—and rightly so—they could be improved upon. That's something I gladly leave to you!

For Further Reading

Beckwith, Francis, William Lane Craig, and James Porter Moreland. *To Everyone an Answer: A Case for the Christian Worldview.* Downers Grove, IL: InterVarsity, 2004.

Craig, William Lane, and Chad V. Meister. *God Is Great, God Is Good: Why Believing in God Is Reasonable and Responsible.* Downers Grove, IL: InterVarsity, 2009.

Guinness, Os. *Unspeakable: Facing Up to Evil in an Age of Genocide and Terror.* San Francisco: HarperOne, 2005.

Kreeft, Peter, and Ronald K. Tacelli. *Handbook of Catholic Apologetics: Reasoned Answers to Questions of Faith.* San Francisco: Ignatius Press, 2009.

Lewis, C. S. *A Grief Observed.* London: HarperCollins, 1994.

_____. *The Problem of Pain.* London: Fount, 1977.

Murray, Michael J., ed. *Reason for the Hope Within.* Grand Rapids: Eerdmans, 1999.

Nicholi, Armand. *The Question of God: C. S. Lewis and Sigmund Freud Debate God, Love, Sex, and the Meaning of Life.* New York: Free Press, 2002.

Sire, James R. *Why Good Arguments Often Fail: Making a More Persuasive Case for Christ.* Downers Grove, IL: InterVarsity, 2006.

Strobel, Lee. *The Case for Faith.* Grand Rapids: Zondervan, 2000.

Zacharias, Ravi, and Norman Geisler, eds. *Who Made God? And Answers to Over 100 Other Tough Questions of Faith.* Grand Rapids: Zondervan, 2003.

9

Conclusion

DEVELOPING YOUR OWN APOLOGETIC APPROACH

Where do you go from here? This book has set out to help you develop your own approach to apologetics. Rather than giving you formulaic answers to all the big questions of faith, I have tried to help you develop your own approach. You need to use approaches and give answers *you* find satisfying. Otherwise, how can you hope to persuade and inform others? My concern throughout this work has been to help you and encourage you to develop an apologetic method, rather than simply presenting you with a list of apologetic answers. It is appropriate to end with some suggestions about how you can further develop your own distinctive approach.

Know Yourself

God made each of us the way we are, and we've got to learn to live with this. We need to appreciate both our weaknesses and our strengths, and work out how to make the best of both. Apologetics is best done in four ways:

1. public speaking
2. writing books
3. personal conversations
4. through the example of our lives and attitudes

Most apologists develop ministries that are based on public speaking, distributed by audio or video recordings. Try to work out what you do best, and work at developing your own distinct approach and voice. Above all, discover the importance of "critical friends" who will help you identify weaknesses and build on your strengths.

You also need to appreciate that doing apologetics can be intellectually and spiritually draining—not because the case for Christianity is weak, but because of the emotional energy we expend in defending and commending it, and our awareness of the importance of this responsibility. C. S. Lewis was acutely aware of this problem, and commented on it:

> I have found that nothing is more dangerous to one's own faith than the work of an apologist. No doctrine of that Faith seems to me so spectral, so unreal as one that I have just successfully defended in a public debate.[1]

Apologists need support if they are to do their work well. You will need fellowship and company. The lone apologist becomes exhausted and weary, partly because of the responsibility of the task. That responsibility is best shared, just as the quality of one's writing and speaking is deepened in dialogue with critical friends—a point to which we now turn.

Learn from Others

It is essential to learn from other apologists. The internet makes available audio presentations from masters of the art, such as leading contemporary American apologists William Lane Craig, Tim Keller, Peter Kreeft, and Ravi Zacharias. Try listening to recordings of their lectures, or reading their books, and analyze their approaches. Some apologists, like Lewis and Tolkien, use novels to develop their apologetics. For example, Marilynne Robinson's novel *Gilead* (2004), which won the Pulitzer Prize for fiction, is a superb exploration of theological themes.

Try to work out how these apologists engage their audiences. What stories do they tell? What illustrations do they use? How do they develop their arguments? How could you develop and adapt their approaches? Understanding their ideas is one thing; being able to adapt and apply them for your own purposes is something quite different.

The idea of "reverse engineering" is helpful here. It refers to the process of examining a product—such as an automobile engine or microchip—with a view to working out how it was designed. Why did the designers choose to do it that way, rather than this way? Can the design be improved? Try reverse engineering an apologetic talk given by an acknowledged expert. See if you can work out what led him to make the various decisions that had to be made in writing that talk. For example, why did he open the talk in that way? What is the implied audience? What factors seem to have shaped his choice of topics? Why did he end the talk as he did? And, most importantly of all: How would *you* do it?

The important thing is that you develop your own apologetic method, adapted to your own gifts on the one hand and your audiences on the other. Reading other apologists is essential to this task. But in the end you will need to create your own answers to questions about faith. Nobody can live on borrowed answers. You will need to develop your own—ones you yourself are happy with. While you can use other people's answers, the best answers are always going to be your own. Why? Because you will have worked them through, fine-tuning them until you are satisfied with them. I have never felt comfortable when using an apologetic approach or giving an apologetic answer I'm not happy with myself, even when I find it used in the writings of leading apologists.

Practice

Finally, remember that apologetics is both a science and an art. It's all about developing a good understanding of the Christian faith and working out how best to connect this with the audience you're engaging. So how do you know how well you're connecting? You need *feedback*—an assessment both honest and affirming, helping you to improve.

At the Oxford Center for Christian Apologetics, students are taught both the theory and practice of apologetics. Knowing the theory makes for a great start, but it's not enough. You need to figure out how to use the ideas you've been exploring. And that means writing short talks and engaging with people's questions—and getting feedback on how you're doing. Our students present their approaches to their peers, who evaluate them and help them craft something even better. It's done in a mutually respectful and supportive manner, which enables students to identify their weaknesses without feeling ashamed and work to minimize them. More importantly, it helps them work out their strengths, and build on them.

What are your strengths? Let's look at some obvious examples. In my own case, I have two particular strengths. First, I used to be an atheist myself. I don't need to be told what it's like; I've been there. I can easily relate to the aggressive atheism of writers such as Richard Dawkins. I know why I left this behind, and can explain this to others. Second, I began my academic life in the natural sciences, both physical and biological, and have kept up-to-date in my reading, including the history and philosophy of science. It means I can have informed and positive conversations with natural scientists who are interested in exploring those important questions of life that lie beyond the scientific method.

We each need to identify our strengths and work out how to use them to our best advantage. For example, Lee Strobel (b. 1952) was a journalist for the *Chicago Tribune*. After his conversion to Christianity, he turned his writing and analytical skills to powerful popular defenses of the Christian faith, including *The Case for Christ* (1998) and *The Case for Faith* (2000). We need to ask what we are good at and how we can use this. After all, remember that Jesus of Nazareth called fishermen by the shores of the Sea of Galilee (Mark 1:16–20) and gave them a new mission—to "fish for people." Their old skills were put to a new and godly use!

In the end, good apologetics is all about practice—both in the sense of *doing something* (as opposed to just thinking about it) and *doing it regularly* (so you get better at it). You can't learn apologetics by reading books or attending classes. It's a skill, not just a matter of acquiring information. The only way to *learn* to construct and deliver apologetic addresses is to construct and deliver apologetic addresses—and get feedback from your peers. If you're not attending a course that incorporates this as part of your preparation, you need to get together with some friends and help each other develop your approaches in this way.

Remember the Inklings? This was a group of writers—including C. S. Lewis and J. R. R. Tolkien—who met regularly in Oxford in the 1930s and 1940s to listen to each other's writing projects and offer constructive criticism. Both The Lord of the Rings and the Chronicles of Narnia series were crafted in this way.[2] Find or form a small circle who want to hone their speaking and writing skills and use them apologetically. There are plenty of people who want to do this, especially at American seminaries and colleges.

And Finally . . .

This short book can never hope to teach you everything about the science and art of apologetics. It can only get you started. Yet hopefully it will have gotten you interested in this field, and helped you to appreciate why apologetics is so stimulating and important. Don't be discouraged if you have found the ideas difficult to master or apply. This book simply maps out the territory. Now it's up to you to explore it in depth and in detail—something that is both fascinating and worthwhile. And how many things in this life are like that?

Notes

Introduction

1. G. K. Chesterton, *Autobiography* (New York: Sheed & Ward, 1936), 229.

Chapter 1 Getting Started

1. The great Swiss theologian Emil Brunner (1889–1966) argued that the gospel rightly caused a "scandal" to modern people on account of doctrines that challenged contemporary myths about human nature and destiny—such as the doctrine of original sin. See Emil Brunner, *The Scandal of Christianity* (Philadelphia: Westminster Press, 1946).

2. C. S. Lewis, "Christian Apologetics," *C. S. Lewis: Essay Collection* (London: Harper-Collins, 2000), 153, 155.

3. David Bosch, *Transforming Mission: Paradigm Shifts in the Theology of Mission* (Maryknoll, NY: Orbis Books, 1991), 11.

4. For useful reflections, see John G. Stackhouse, *Humble Apologetics: Defending the Faith Today* (Oxford: Oxford University Press, 2002), 131–205.

5. Blaise Pascal, *Pensées* (Mineola, NY: Dover Publications, 2003), 52.

Chapter 2 Apologetics and Contemporary Culture

1. Edward John Carnell, *An Introduction to Christian Apologetics* (Grand Rapids: Eerdmans, 1948). For an analysis, see Kenneth C. Harper, "Edward John Carnell: An Evaluation of His Apologetics," *Journal of the Evangelical Theological Society* 20 (1977), 133–46.

2. Kevin Vanhoozer, "Theology and the Condition of Postmodernity," in *The Cambridge Companion to Postmodern Theology*, ed. Kevin Vanhoozer (Cambridge: Cambridge University Press, 2003), 3–24.

3. Lewis, "Christian Apologetics," *C. S. Lewis: Essay Collection* (London: HarperCollins, 2000), 151.

Chapter 3 The Theological Basis of Apologetics

1. Avery Dulles, *A History of Apologetics*, 3rd ed. (San Francisco: Ignatius Press, 2005), xix.

2. Richard S. Westfall, *The Life of Isaac Newton* (Cambridge: Cambridge University Press, 1993), 73–75.

3. For some important representative accounts, see Colin E. Gunton, *The Actuality of Atonement: A Study of Metaphor, Rationality, and the Christian Tradition* (Grand Rapids: Eerdmans, 1989); Charles E. Hill and Frank A. James, eds., *The Glory of the Atonement:*

Biblical, Historical & Practical Perspectives (Downers Grove, IL: InterVarsity, 2004); Peter Schmiechen, *Saving Power: Theories of Atonement and Forms of the Church* (Grand Rapids: Eerdmans, 2005); and Thomas F. Torrance, *Atonement: The Person and Work of Christ* (Downers Grove, IL: InterVarsity, 2009).

4. Lewis, "Christian Apologetics," *C. S. Lewis: Essay Collection* (London: HarperCollins, 2000), 152–53.

5. For an excellent introduction, which offers the apologist many helpful approaches and analogies, see Cornelius Plantinga, *Not the Way It's Supposed to Be: A Breviary of Sin* (Grand Rapids: Eerdmans, 1995).

6. C. S. Lewis, *Mere Christianity* (London: HarperCollins, 2002), 63.

Chapter 4 The Importance of the Audience

1. James C. Walters, "Paul, Adoption, and Inheritance," *Paul in the Greco-Roman World*, ed. J. Paul Sampley (Harrisburg, PA: Trinity Press International, 2003), 42–76.

2. See Romans 8:15, 23; 9:4; Galatians 4:5; Ephesians 1:5.

3. See the classic study of Robert F. Zehnle, *Peter's Pentecost Discourse: Tradition and Lucan Reinterpretation in Peter's Speeches of Acts 2 and 3* (Nashville: Abingdon, 1971). Although dated in some respects, the work remains an important analysis of the text itself and its underlying strategy.

4. See W. S. Kurz, "Hellenistic Rhetoric in the Christological Proofs of Luke-Acts," *Catholic Biblical Quarterly* 42 (1980), 171–95.

5. See the classic study of Bertil Gartner, *The Areopagus Speech and Natural Revelation* (Uppsala: Gleerup, 1955).

6. Ittai Gradel, *Emperor Worship and Roman Religion* (Oxford: Oxford University Press, 2002).

7. See the important analysis in Bruce W. Winter, "Official Proceedings and the Forensic Speeches in Acts 24–26," *The Book of Acts: Ancient Literary Setting*, ed. B. W. Winter and A. D. Clarke (Grand Rapids: Eerdmans, 1994), 305–36.

Chapter 5 The Reasonableness of the Christian Faith

1. C. S. Lewis, "Is Theology Poetry?" *C. S. Lewis: Essay Collection* (London: Harper-Collins, 2000), 21.

2. Austin Farrer, "In His Image," *Remembering C. S. Lewis*, ed. James T. Como (San Francisco: Ignatius Press, 2005), 344–45.

3. Letter of 1949 to Edward Sackville-West, cited in Michael de-la-Noy, *Eddy: The Life of Edward Sackville-West* (London: Bodley Head, 1988), 237.

4. See, for example, Alasdair MacIntyre, *Whose Justice? Which Rationality?* (London: Duckworth, 1988); Stephen Toulmin, *Cosmopolis: The Hidden Agenda of Modernity* (New York: Free Press, 1990); John Gray, *Enlightenment's Wake: Politics and Culture at the Close of the Modern Age* (London: Routledge, 1995).

5. William James, "The Sentiment of Rationality," *The Will to Believe and Other Essays in Popular Philosophy* (New York: Longmans, Green, and Co., 1897), 63–110.

6. See Michael J. Sandel, *Justice: What's the Right Thing to Do?* (New York: Farrar, Straus and Giroux, 2010).

7. Stephen Toulmin, *The Uses of Argument* (Cambridge: Cambridge University Press, 1958), 183.

8. MacIntyre, *Whose Justice?*, 6.

9. Isaiah Berlin, *Concepts and Categories: Philosophical Essays* (New York: Viking Press, 1979), 2–5, 161–62.

10. Terry Eagleton, "Lunging, Flailing, Mispunching: A Review of Richard Dawkins's *The God Delusion*," *London Review of Books*, October 19, 2006.

11. Alvin Plantinga, *God and Other Minds: A Study of the Rational Justification of Belief in God* (Ithaca, NY: Cornell University Press, 1990).

12. Richard Rorty, "Pragmatism, Relativism, and Irrationalism," *Proceedings and Addresses of the American Philosophical Association* 53 (1980): 719–38, quote at p. 730.

13. Julia Kristeva, *The Incredible Need to Believe* (New York: Columbia University Press, 2009), 3.

14. Christopher Hitchens, *God Is Not Great: How Religion Poisons Everything* (New York: Twelve, 2007), 5. For criticism of this approach, see Alister McGrath, *Why God Won't Go Away: Is the New Atheism Running on Empty?* (Nashville: Thomas Nelson, 2011).

15. C. S. Lewis, "On Obstinacy in Belief," *C. S. Lewis: Essay Collection* (London: Harper-Collins, 2000), 213–14.

16. Jonathan Edwards, *The Works of Jonathan Edwards*, vol. 1 (Edinburgh: Banner of Truth Trust, 1974), 290.

17. Ibid.

18. Austin Farrer, "The Christian Apologist," *Light on C. S. Lewis*, ed. Jocelyn Gibb (London: Geoffrey Bles, 1965), 26.

19. Ibid.

20. Simone Weil, *First and Last Notebooks* (London: Oxford University Press, 1970), 147.

21. Brian Leftow, "From Jerusalem to Athens," *God and the Philosophers*, ed. Thomas V. Morris (Oxford: Oxford University Press, 1994), 191.

22. John Polkinghorne, *Theology in the Context of Science* (London: SPCK, 2008), 85–86.

23. C. S. Lewis, *Surprised by Joy* (London: HarperCollins, 2002), 197.

24. Richard Dawkins, *River out of Eden: A Darwinian View of Life* (London: Phoenix, 1995), 133.

25. See, for example, Alvin Plantinga, "Reason and Belief in God," *Faith and Philosophy: Reason and Belief in God*, ed. Alvin Plantinga and Nicholas Wolterstorff (Notre Dame, IN: University of Notre Dame Press, 1983), 16–93.

26. Isaiah Berlin, *The Crooked Timber of Humanity: Chapters in the History of Ideas* (London: Pimlico, 2003), 208–13. The curious title of this important collection of essays reflects a famous dictum of Immanuel Kant: "Nothing straight was ever made out of the crooked timber of humanity."

27. See M. Neil Browne and Stuart M. Keeley, *Asking the Right Questions: A Guide to Critical Thinking*, 8th ed. (Upper Saddle River, NJ: Pearson Prentice Hall, 2007), 196.

28. Charles S. Peirce, *Collected Papers*, vol. 5, ed. Charles Hartshorne and Paul Weiss (Cambridge, MA: Harvard University Press, 1960), 189. I reflect further on the importance of this approach in Alister E. McGrath, *Surprised by Meaning: Science, Faith, and How We Make Sense of Things* (Louisville: Westminster John Knox), 2011.

29. Ibid.

30. The best studies are Paul Humphreys, *The Chances of Explanation: Causal Explanation in the Social, Medical, and Physical Sciences* (Princeton: Princeton University Press, 1989); and James Woodward, *Making Things Happen: A Theory of Causal Explanation* (Oxford: Oxford University Press, 2003).

31. For a good discussion of Aquinas on this point, see William E. Carroll, "Divine Agency, Contemporary Physics, and the Autonomy of Nature," *Heythrop Journal* 49 (2008): 582–602.

32. Helge S. Kragh, *Conceptions of Cosmos: From Myths to the Accelerating Universe: A History of Cosmology* (Oxford: Oxford University Press, 2006).

33. See especially Peter Lipton, *Inference to the Best Explanation*, 2nd ed. (London: Routledge, 2004).

34. Richard Swinburne, *The Existence of God*, 2nd ed. (Oxford: Clarendon Press, 2004).

35. Michael Friedman, "Explanation and Scientific Understanding," *Journal of Philosophy* 71 (1974): 5–19; Paul Kitcher, "Explanatory Unification and the Causal Structure of the World," *Scientific Explanation*, ed. P. Kitcher and W. Salmon (Minneapolis: University of Minnesota Press, 1989), 410–505.

36. For example, Margaret Morrison, *Unifying Scientific Theories: Physical Concepts and Mathematical Structures* (Cambridge: Cambridge University Press, 2000).

37. Terry Eagleton, *Reason, Faith, and Revolution: Reflections on the God Debate* (New Haven: Yale University Press, 2009), 28.

38. William S. Bainbridge and Rodney Stark, *The Future of Religion: Secularization, Revival, and Cult Formation* (Berkeley: University of California Press, 1985), 1.

39. Richard Shweder, "Atheists Agonistes," *New York Times*, November 27, 2006.

40. Ibid.

41. A point famously emphasized by Karl R. Popper, *The Poverty of Historicism* (London: Routledge & Kegan Paul, 1957).

42. Eagleton, *Reason, Faith, and Revolution*, 87–89.

43. J. R. R. Tolkien, "Mythopoeia," *Tree and Leaf* (London: HarperCollins, 1992), 85–90; quote at p. 89.

44. See especially Walter Schmithals, *The Theology of the First Christians* (Louisville: Westminster John Knox, 1997), 122–23, 146–51. See further Raymond Pickett, *The Cross in Corinth: The Social Significance of the Death of Jesus* (Sheffield, England: Sheffield Academic Press, 1997), 213–16; and Edward Adams and David G. Horrell, eds., *Christianity at Corinth: The Quest for the Pauline Church* (Louisville: Westminster John Knox, 2004).

Chapter 6 Pointers to Faith

1. Augustine of Hippo, *Confessions* VII.x.16.

2. Helge Kragh, *Cosmology and Controversy* (Princeton: Princeton University Press, 1999), 262.

3. For a thorough exploration of the scientific issues and their apologetic implications, see Alister E. McGrath, *A Fine-Tuned Universe: The Quest for God in Science and Theology* (Louisville: Westminster John Knox, 2009), 109–201.

4. Richard Swinburne, "The Argument from the Fine-Tuning of the Universe," *Physical Cosmology and Philosophy*, ed. John Leslie (New York: Macmillan, 1990), 154–73; Robin Collins, "A Scientific Argument for the Existence of God: The Fine-Tuning Design Argument," *Reason for the Hope Within*, ed. Michael J. Murray (Grand Rapids: Eerdmans, 1999), 47–75.

5. Martin J. Rees, *Just Six Numbers: The Deep Forces That Shape the Universe* (London: Phoenix, 2000).

6. Robert J. Spitzer, *New Proofs for the Existence of God: Contributions of Contemporary Physics and Philosophy* (Grand Rapids: Eerdmans, 2010), 60–65.

7. Fred Hoyle, "The Universe: Past and Present Reflections," *Annual Review of Astronomy and Astrophysics* 20 (1982): 16.

8. Spitzer, *New Proofs for the Existence of God*, 34–42.

9. Heinz R. Pagels, *The Cosmic Code: Quantum Physics and the Language of Nature* (Harmondsworth: Penguin, 1984), 83.

10. Paul Davies, *The Mind of God: Science and the Search for Ultimate Meaning* (London: Penguin, 1992), 77.

11. John Polkinghorne, *Science and Creation: The Search for Understanding* (London: SPCK, 1988), 20–21.

12. Eugene Wigner, "The Unreasonable Effectiveness of Mathematics," *Communications on Pure and Applied Mathematics* 13 (1960): 1–14.

13. C. S. Lewis, *Miracles* (New York: Macmillan, 1947), 26.

14. Charles A. Coulson, *Science and Christian Belief* (Chapel Hill: University of North Carolina Press, 1958), 22.

15. Augustine, *On the Trinity* XVI.iv.6.

16. Audio recording available at http://media.premier.org.uk/misc/4b519ce0-5a9e-4b1d-86ca-8def12ebd5c1.mp3.

17. Paul Kurtz, *Forbidden Fruit: The Ethics of Humanism* (Buffalo: Prometheus Books, 1988), 65.

18. Richard Rorty, *Contingency, Irony, and Solidarity* (Cambridge: Cambridge University Press, 1989), 194 n.6.

19. Richard Rorty, *The Consequences of Pragmatism* (Minneapolis: University of Minnesota Press, 1982), xlii.

20. Ibid.

21. C. S. Lewis, *Mere Christianity* (London: HarperCollins, 2002), 3–8.

22. Ibid., 24.

23. C. S. Lewis, *The Abolition of Man* (London: Collins, 1978), 19.

24. Philip E. Devine, *Natural Law Ethics* (Westport, CT: Greenwood, 2000), 32–34.

25. Augustine, *Confessions* I.i.1.

26. Blaise Pascal, *Pensées* (Mineola, NY: Dover Publications, 2003), 113.

27. Ibid.

28. See Lewis, *Mere Christianity*, 134–38. See also a similar argument in C. S. Lewis, "The Weight of Glory," *Screwtape Proposes a Toast* (London: Collins, 1965), 94–110.

29. For Lewis's approach, see Peter Kreeft, "C. S. Lewis's Argument from Desire," *G. K. Chesterton and C. S. Lewis: The Riddle of Joy*, ed. Michael H. MacDonald and Andrew A. Tadie (Grand Rapids: Eerdmans, 1989), 249–72. More generally, see John Haldane, "Philosophy, the Restless Heart, and the Meaning of Theism," *Ratio* 19 (2006): 421–40.

30. Augustine, *Confessions* I.i.1.

31. Lewis, *Mere Christianity*, 136–37.

32. Charles Taylor, *A Secular Age* (Cambridge, MA: Harvard University Press, 2007), 530.

33. Avihu Zakai, "Jonathan Edwards and the Language of Nature: The Re-Enchantment of the World in the Age of Scientific Reasoning," *Journal of Religious History* 26 (2002): 15–41.

34. Lewis, *Mere Christianity*, 1.

35. Lewis, "Weight of Glory," 94–110.

36. Ibid., 97.

37. Ibid.

38. Ibid., 98.

39. Ibid., 105.

40. Ibid., 100.

41. Ibid., 106.

42. Ibid., 108.

43. Ibid., 107–8.

44. Ibid., 107.

45. See Paul Elmer More, *Christ the Word* (Princeton: Princeton University Press, 1927).

46. Lisa Miller, *Heaven: Our Enduring Fascination with the Afterlife* (New York: HarperCollins, 2010).

47. John Cottingham, *Why Believe?* (London: Continuum, 2009), 47.

48. For comment, see the classic studies of Edward A. Dowey, *The Knowledge of God in Calvin's Theology* (New York: Columbia University Press, 1952); and T. H. L. Parker, *Calvin's Doctrine of the Knowledge of God* (Edinburgh: Oliver & Boyd, 1969).

Chapter 7 Gateways for Apologetics

1. Peter Brown, *Augustine of Hippo* (London: Faber & Faber, 1967).

2. Augustine, *Confessions* V.xiii.23–xiv.25.

3. James Robert Brown, *Philosophy of Mathematics: An Introduction to the World of Proofs and Pictures* (London: Routledge, 1999, 71–78); George Boolos, "Gödel's Second Incompleteness Theorem Explained in Words of One Syllable," *Mind* 103 (1994): 1–3.

4. For a highly influential discussion, see John Lucas, "Minds, Machines and Gödel," *Philosophy* 36 (1961): 112–27.

5. For two good assessments of Schaeffer's approach, see Thomas V. Morris, *Francis Schaeffer's Apologetics: A Critique* (Grand Rapids: Baker, 1987); Bryan A. Follis, *Truth with Love: Apologetics of Francis Schaeffer* (Wheaton: Crossway, 2006).

6. Francis Schaeffer, *The God Who Is There*, *Complete Works of Francis Schaeffer*, vol. 1 (Westchester, IL: Crossway, 1982), 130.

7. Ibid., 134.

8. For a good analysis, see Morris, *Francis Schaeffer's Apologetics*, 21–22.

9. Schaeffer, *The God Who Is There*, 132.

10. Ibid., 140.

11. Ibid., 110.

12. C. S. Lewis, *Surprised by Joy* (London: HarperCollins, 2002), 138.

13. C. S. Lewis, *Rehabilitations and Other Essays* (London: Oxford University Press, 1939), 158.

14. See Roy Baumeister, *Meanings of Life* (New York: Guilford Press, 1991). Baumeister's analysis of the importance of questions of identity, value, purpose, and agency is of major importance to Christian apologetics.

15. Hans Frei, *The Eclipse of Biblical Narrative: A Study in Eighteenth and Nineteenth Century Biblical Hermeneutics* (New Haven: Yale University Press, 1977).

16. Alasdair MacIntyre, *After Virtue* (London: Duckworth, 1985), 216.

17. Baumeister, *Meanings of Life*.

18. N. T. Wright, "How Can the Bible Be Authoritative?" *Vox Evangelica* 21 (1991): 7–32.

19. N. T. Wright, *The New Testament and the People of God* (Minneapolis: Fortress, 1992), 132.

20. See Verlyn Flieger, *Splintered Light: Logos and Language in Tolkien's World* (Kent, OH: Kent State University, 2002); Jeffrey L. Morrow, "J. R. R. Tolkien as a Christian for Our Times," *Evangelical Review of Theology* 29 (2005), 164–77.

21. Dan Brown, *The Da Vinci Code: A Novel* (New York: Doubleday, 2003), 233.

22. Brown is totally wrong on all these points. See, for example, Bart D. Ehrman, *Truth and Fiction in The Da Vinci Code: A Historian Reveals What We Really Know About Jesus, Mary Magdalene, and Constantine* (Oxford: Oxford University Press, 2004), 23–24.

23. The best account of the fabrication of this myth is Massimo Introvigne, *Gli Illuminati e il Priorato di Sion* (Milan: Piemme, 2005). An English summary of this work is available at http://www.cesnur.org/2005/pa_introvigne.htm.

24. Philip Pullman, *The Good Man Jesus and the Scoundrel Christ* (Edinburgh: Canongate, 2010).

25. You might enjoy reading the interesting study of William G. Johnson and Marcia K. Houtman, "Platonic Shadows in C. S. Lewis' Narnia Chronicles," *Modern Fiction Studies* 32 (1986), 75–87.

26. For a detailed discussion, see Gail Fine, *Plato on Knowledge and Forms: Selected Essays* (Oxford: Oxford University Press, 2003).

27. James C. Walters, "Paul, Adoption, and Inheritance," *Paul in the Greco-Roman World*, ed. J. Paul Sampley (Harrisburg, PA: Trinity Press International, 2003), 42–76.

28. Simone Weil, *The Need for Roots* (London: Routledge, 2002), 43.

29. Walter Brueggemann, *The Land: Place as Gift, Promise, and Challenge in Biblical Faith*, 2nd ed. (Philadelphia: Fortress Press, 2002), 1.

30. Bill Carter, "Why 'Cheers' Proved So Intoxicating," *New York Times*, Sunday, May 9, 1993.

31. Philip D. Kenneson, "There's No Such Thing as Objective Truth, and It's a Good Thing, Too," *Christian Apologetics in the Postmodern World*, ed. Timothy R. Phillips and Dennis L. Okholm (Downers Grove, IL: InterVarsity Press, 1995), 155–70.

Chapter 8 Questions about Faith

1. For apologetic motifs in the New Testament, see Avery Dulles, *A History of Apologetics* (San Francisco: Ignatius Press, 2005), 1–25.

2. One of the best is the comprehensive account by Peter Kreeft and Ronald K. Tacelli, *Handbook of Catholic Apologetics: Reasoned Answers to Questions of Faith* (San Francisco: Ignatius Press, 2009). Every apologist can learn much from this work.

3. My discussion of the different approaches of Martin Luther and C. S. Lewis to suffering is relevant here: Alister McGrath, "The Cross, Suffering, and Theological Bewilderment: Reflections on Martin Luther and C. S. Lewis," *The Passionate Intellect: Christian Faith and the Discipleship of the Mind* (Downers Grove, IL: InterVarsity, 2010), 57–69.

4. Dorothy L. Sayers, *Creed or Chaos?* (New York, Harcourt Brace, 1949), 4.

5. Sigmund Freud, *The Future of an Illusion* (New York: Norton, 1961), 42.

6. Sigmund Freud, *Civilization and its Discontents* (New York: Norton, 1962), 21. The official English translation of the title of this work is not quite correct; it is better translated as "Anxiety in Culture" (*Das Unbehagen in der Kultur*).

7. See Armand Nicholi, *The Question of God: C. S. Lewis and Sigmund Freud Debate God, Love, Sex, and the Meaning of Life* (New York: Free Press, 2002).

8. C. S. Lewis, *Surprised by Joy* (London: HarperCollins, 2002), 265.

9. Freud, *Future of an Illusion*, 35.

10. C. S. Lewis, *The Problem of Pain* (London: HarperCollins, 2002), 91.

Chapter 9 Conclusion

1. C. S. Lewis, "Christian Apologetics," *C. S. Lewis: Essay Collection* (London: Harper-Collins, 2000), 159.

2. See Humphrey Carpenter, *The Inklings: C. S. Lewis, J. R. R. Tolkien, Charles Williams, and Their Friends* (Boston: Allen and Unwin, 1978); Diana Glyer, *The Company They Keep: C. S. Lewis and J. R. R. Tolkien as Writers in Community* (Kent, OH: Kent State University Press, 2007).

Index

Alister McGrath is president of the Oxford Center for Christian Apologetics, and professor of theology, ministry, and education at King's College, London. Before moving to London, McGrath was professor of historical theology at Oxford University. A former atheist, McGrath has a longstanding interest in the effective and faithful commendation of the Christian faith to secular culture, and has been a significant voice in the Christian response to the "New Atheism" of Richard Dawkins and Christopher Hitchens. His best-known apologetic books include *The Dawkins Delusion?* (2007) and *Why God Won't Go Away* (2011). He has also published many bestselling textbooks on Christian theology, including *Christian Theology: An Introduction* (5th ed., 2010) and *The Christian Theology Reader* (4th ed., 2011).